MAGGIE KUHN
ON AGING

MAGGIE KUHN
ON AGING

A Dialogue edited by
Dieter Hessel

The Westminster Press
Philadelphia

First edition

PUBLISHED BY THE WESTMINSTER PRESS®

PHILADELPHIA, PENNSYLVANIA

Printed in the United States of America

9 8 7 6 5 4 3 2 1

Library of Congress Cataloging in Publication Data

Hessel, Dieter T
  Maggie Kuhn on aging.

  Bibliography: p.
  1. Old age. 2. Retirement—United States.
3. Aged—United States. I. Kuhn, Margaret E.,
joint author. II. Title.
HQ1064.U5H47   301.43'5'0973   77–24294
ISBN 0–664–24146–8

To the Gray Panthers—old, young, and middle-aged—whose revolutionary life-style humanizes and heals

CONTENTS

PREFACE

In the '60s the most articulate young activists were described as forerunners of a new society. They set the pace in social criticism and experimented with new forms of community, only to fall silent when policies and institutions failed to yield. Now, in the '70s, another group of adults show signs of being the real forerunners of social change. This group is the growing number of older persons (often active in the church) who refuse to accept "sociogenic aging"—an assigned role as nonpersons whom society would relegate to warehouses and playpens.

Margaret E. Kuhn, better known as Maggie, is one of the most outspoken leaders of older Americans. She has been ahead of both church and society for a long time. In 1972 she convened the Gray Panthers for the purpose of liberating older persons from "paternalism and oppression with which society keeps us powerless." The group began as a nationally organized consultation of older and younger adults for social change. The philosophy of that activist group has often been ignored in the church's own ministry with the aging. This despite the fact that Maggie Kuhn served the church professionally for twenty-five years as a program executive responsible for social education and action.

I first met Maggie when she was on sabbatical teaching a course where I was completing graduate study. She made me aware that being a church "bureaucrat" could be quite rewarding. Soon we found ourselves on the same national staff but with separate responsibilities. Here at last we can collaborate on a special project.

On behalf of an ecumenical group who develop Christian Education: Shared Approaches, I asked Maggie to write an action guide on aging. (The particular educational approach for which this book was written is described in *A Manual for Doing the Word;* Philadelphia: United Church Press.) It would focus attention on such questions as: Do the aging have a significant ministry in church and community? What can be the witness and service *of* older Christians beyond the conventional ministries of the church *to, for,* and *with,* the aging? This Dialogue with Maggie Kuhn on aging will provoke task forces, study groups, and program committees to reexamine their assumptions about what older persons want, need, and can do.

The church has some distance to go if it is to take her approach to the subject more seriously and reform ministry accordingly. The church already has more older persons than the society as a whole. (Approximately one fourth of the members of main-line denominations are over age sixty-five!) Heavily involved with community programs, retirement housing, and nursing homes, the church still arbitrarily retires its professionals at age sixty-five. Changes in the church's own policies and programs along the lines advocated in this Dialogue would certainly help to set the pace for the larger society.

Maggie embodies a new philosophy of living whole when old. She is not asking everyone to try looking or acting younger; rather she is asking all to act their age as persons concerned for justice, confident of wisdom, open to self-discovery, ready to risk self-direction. She knows that not everyone reaches old age with her social action experience and enthusiasm for social change. But Maggie also knows that we have been wrongly taught that old is a condition of loss, a time to quit, a mandate to withdraw. Can we demonstrate that old age is not a defeat, but a victory; not a punishment, but a privilege?

> Unless we are old already, the next "old people" will be us. Whether we go along with the kind of treatment meted out to those who are now old depends upon how far society can sell us the bill of goods it sold them—and it depends more upon that than upon any research. No pill or regime known, or likely, could transform the latter years of life as fully as could a change in our vision of age and a militancy in attaining that change. (Alex Comfort, *A Good Age*, pp. 13–14.)

This Dialogue results from an intensive one-week course involving a group of twelve ministers and one laywoman who enrolled in San Francisco Theological Seminary's Advanced Pastoral Studies Program. Their basic text was Robert N. Butler, *Why Survive? Being Old in America* (Harper & Row, Publishers, Inc., 1975), which makes excellent companion reading with this Dialogue. The students came from nine states—three were from Hawaii, two from Florida. They ranged in age from a pastor under age thirty to one nearing age sixty. There were Caucasians, Japanese, and Chinese. John Hadsell, director of the Advanced Pastoral Studies Program, gave permission for us to develop this printed resource. The course sessions were taped by Richard Mesiavech. Transcript editing was assisted by Barbara Surbrook. The Bibliography was prepared by Jean Hopper, librarian of the Gray Panther National Staff, Philadelphia. Audio-visual suggestions were compiled by Robert McClel-

lan, associate Pastor of the Point Loma Community Presbyterian Church, San Diego, California. Basic research for the
chapter on mandatory retirement was provided by Rosalie
Schofield, of the Gray Panther National Staff.

The cast of characters in the following chapters is:

M—Maggie Kuhn

S—Students in the Advanced Pastoral Studies Program

E—Editor

I enjoyed editing the manuscript and relish the hours
spent with the author in that special camaraderie of persons
who share a social change commitment. We hope that you
will share it too.

DIETER T. HESSEL
Program Agency
The United Presbyterian Church U.S.A.

I.

INTRODUCTION—
AGE IN A NEW AGE

Agism is the notion that people become inferior because they have lived a specified number of years.—**M. K.**

M: This is a new age—an age of liberation, self-determination, and freedom. Winds of change are blowing from every quarter, disturbing every system, every organization, every human group. None of us can escape or hide from them.

Some groups have been unmoored, shaken, damaged by these changes. Some are resisting them. Some have been liberated by them. In this age of self-determination and liberation many groups are struggling for freedom. Their struggles are all of a piece:

> The nonwhites struggling against racism
> The women struggling against the domination of men and sexism
> The young and the old struggling against agism
> The developing nations in the Third World struggling against U.S. imperialism and Pax Americana

All these struggles are linked in the worldwide struggle for a new humanity. Together they have the potential of a new community-based social justice system of human compassion and selfhood. Old people have a large stake in this new community—in helping to create it and extend it. The winds of change are impelling and empowering. They can free us or destroy us.

As liberated spirits we can shake off our old hang-ups and prejudices, heal ourselves of the brain damage that society has done to our heads, free ourselves and our society from some social fictions about getting old and being old:

1. Old age is bad, a personal and social disaster.
2. Old age is a disease that nobody will admit to having.
3. Old age is disengagement from responsibility. It often begins with enforced retirement, a shock that some people never get over because they equate it with retirement from life.
4. Old age is mindless. Time for play and naps when the mind stops functioning and regresses to senility, relieved only by bingo and soap operas.
5. Old age is sexless, with denial of our own sexuality.

To free ourselves from these "myths," we need to find and affirm wholly new images of ourselves and take on entirely new roles—new to Western society. We need to counter the old dehumanizing images of old age with new ones that enable us to be comfortable with our bodies. We need to continue to grow, learn, and keep our minds and spirits vibrant as long as we live.

We are not "senior citizens" or "golden-agers." We are the elders, the experienced ones; we are maturing, growing adults responsible for the survival of our society. We are not wrinkled babies, succumbing to trivial, purposeless waste of our years and our time.

We are a new breed of old people. There are more of us alive today than at any other time in history. We are better educated, healthier, with more at stake in this society. We are redefining goals, taking stock of our skills and experience, looking to the future.

Erik Erikson speaks of old age as "a time of integrity," of

absolute honesty in an age that has lost its way, in terms of deception, double-dealing, corruption in high and low places. Old age is also a time of great fulfillment—personal fulfillment, when all the loose ends of life can be gathered together.

I'd like to elaborate just a little on the wastefulness of our society, what I call the "Detroit" syndrome. The Detroit syndrome builds obsolescence into all our thinking and production. Only the new model is desirable, marketable, profitable. The "Detroit" mentality has taken us over as a society. We are a wasteful society. We've been wasting people in Indochina, and we've been wasting people who cannot produce at what we consider to be productive peaks. They're surplus, they're scrap. We as a society, for all our protestations of compassion and humanity, have never come to grips with dependency and been able to deal with it in any human, compassionate way. We make the people who are dependent non-people. We throw away people, and before we throw them away we warehouse them in institutions. We make them vegetables, fit for nothing but scrap piles.

Our society is agist, in case you hadn't received the message. It is also racist and sexist. *Agism* is the arbitrary discrimination against people on the basis of their chronological age. Agism, in this new age of self-determination, is a crucial problem of alienation and oppression for the religious community of America. The churches and the synagogues have yet to come to grips with it. In our collective ministries we represent a substantial toehold in the growing population of Americans who are sixty-five and older. I'll cite some statistics to back this up. You do know that there are more than 23,000,000 people sixty-five and over now in the United States. Sylvia Porter reports a study that the U.S. Department of Health, Education and Welfare asked the Center for the Study of Democratic Institutions in Santa Barbara to perform. The study was so disquieting to the Department that they tried to suppress the figures and discount Sylvia Porter's reporting of them. In round numbers the study showed that by the year 2000, just over twenty years from now, 1 out of every 3 Americans will be sixty-five or over. That's a large segment of society, even if the proportions are overstated. If you are over forty, you are going to be in that segment. Nearly half of the United States' population is going to be age fifty and over by the year 2000. If we continue to scrap pile people at our going rate, our society is going to be really sick—in fact, it will be dying. We've got twenty years of grace, and we'd better make the most of them.

I propose to attempt to challenge the present mind-set of the church that is largely accommodative to the existing wasteful system. Most of the things that old people need, all people need: food, clothing, shelter, medical care, friends, adequate income, and purpose in living. We've done a good job of social analysis, so there's a long laundry list of needs. And the list gets longer. Having done that analysis, we look at our congregations. Many people over fifty are church members. The church responds to the elderly principally in terms of custodial care in retirement homes and accommodation to the existing order. Custodial care in most church-related homes is expensive. Expensive to get in, expensive to stay in, expensive to maintain. But demeaning, because the inmates (and they often are just inmates) have little to say about that home—its governance, its quality of life, its programs. And yet it is their home. Well-meaning governing boards make the residents even more powerless than they are. They don't come to retirement homes until they're on their last legs, but they still have minds and spirit. (The average age is something like eighty-two.) The point is that church-related homes are highly paternalistic—administered by well-meaning professionals, good people, but making the powerless still more abject. The churches have bought heavily not only into the "home" syndrome (the custodial care of people) but also into the "services and recreation" syndrome: "Golden Age Clubs," which I call glorified playpens. That's extravagant language and I mean it to be. They trivialize old age, assuming that all that people want to do in their old age is to play—just one round of merriment after another. Many of my peers are conditioned to believe that they deserve to play after years of hard work.

How does this prepare anyone to deal with the angst that is within us all about growing old? The sheer terror of not having enough money, of acquiring some crippling disease, cannot be dispensed with fun and games. One old man said to me, with some disgust: "My God, I've made ashtrays for everybody I know. Can I give you an ashtray?" This is not to downgrade play, but play on these terms is such a waste —again, the Detroit syndrome. It's a waste of experience, of years of being able to cope. Play does not help us to develop positive new images of strength. Some churches are providing services: Meals On Wheels, friendly visiting, transportation, etc. Services are fine; they are needed, but they won't change the prevailing value system. They won't really change the basic social structures that are sick, sick unto death.

We have extended life. At the turn of the century, people lived an average of from forty-four to forty-five years. Now, according to the 1970 census, the life-span is roughly 70.4 years, which is a great big shift. The population of the group sixty-five years and older is 23,000,000 more than 10 percent of the total population of the United States. The percentage of church members over age sixty is at least twice as high. Because the aged make up a significant group in terms of the total population, I would like at this point to give you a few general facts about the group as a whole.

There are 68.7 males per 100 females for the white group, and 72.9 males per 100 females for the black group. Over 70 percent of the males in this age group are living with their wives. The rest are widowed, divorced, or single. Only 37.6 percent of the females in this age group are living with their husbands. Of the rest, more than half are widowed. The living arrangements of this age category are as follows: over 95 percent of the males live in households, with their wives or someone else. About 5 percent do not live in a household. About 94 percent of the females live in a household, with their husbands or someone else. About 5.6 percent do not live in a household. The median income of families in this age category was $7,298 (1974), which was three fifths (.57) of the median income of all families, $12,836. However, 10 percent of those living as family heads were below poverty level; for unrelated individuals, almost 32 percent were below poverty level.

In certain places, like Florida, Southern California, Nebraska, and Iowa, the proportion of population over age sixty is between 12 and 15 percent; and in some counties in Florida it may be up to 40 percent. In twenty years many more places across the country will have such proportions of older persons. In the year 2000 conservative estimates are that people over sixty will constitute 20 to 35 percent of the overall population.

S: Why the high figures for Nebraska and Iowa?

M: Well, it's curious. Those are agricultural states, with farms that have been in the family for a number of years. In other agricultural states the family farms have disappeared. So where there are vestigial remains of the family farm, there is an old population that is stable. In many of the older cities in the East, particularly in the declining sections, large proportions of elderly may be found. Most of those people are very poor and live below the federal figures for subsistence; but they have no place to go, property values being what they are. It's very interesting to see what our society has become. We're not a youthful nation anymore. We will soon be a middle-aged nation.

S: Another factor related to that, at least in Iowa, is that Iowa has not grown in population. The younger ones leave the state to seek education and employment elsewhere.

M: And the older people stay behind and hold on to the farm, if they're still farming.

S: For the older ones, the pattern more often is to move into town and buy one of the older houses in town.

M: But in most instances they do not move out of the state. They live close to the land, close to their own roots. This gives those states more stability and historical continuity. If people could still stay close to the land, the situation in urban America might be very different. We've violated the continuum of life by our age-segregated life-styles and economic structures, and we've violated the whole created order. We have created a plastic world, a man-made environment, with extravagant use of resources. This plastic world is a substitute for a real environment.

S: Are you saying that people should stay on their farms?

M: Well, I get worried about agribusiness.

S: Agribusiness is for young farmers. They expect the same kind of pace out of a young farmer that a production line expects in Detroit. One of the neat things about family farming was that the elder of the tribe could go to town, and still come back and putter around the land and work during planting time and harvesttime at his own pace. He was never cut off the way a factory worker is. But with these agribusinesses, a farmer gets to retirement age and no one wants to see him around anymore. It's just like the factory.

M: A number of people in the Gray Panther movement [see Preface] are Good Earth people. We believe that this is another kind of coalition that old people should be encouraged to support. As good stewards of the earth and the created order we should be working hand in glove with the environmentalists. It will take that kind of cooperative effort to fight off the powerful interests that say that we can't protect the environment and have jobs. In the short haul we probably won't, but in the longer haul we must or we will not survive. Family farmers and Good Earth people alike know that environmental protection is good for business, though not for quick profits. Why do we ignore the inherited wisdom?

S: I'd like to talk about old people in our cities. They are pretty isolated in declining neighborhoods. They are often the victims of crime, easy targets for young toughs. They stay on in old neighborhoods in homes which they own but cannot afford to keep in good repair. They can't afford to move, either, or to pay the increasing taxes and electric bills.

M: You are describing a sad situation that is all too common in cities, even in older suburbs. I suspect that many isolated old people are still on the membership rolls of a church. They don't keep up their pledges or church attendance, and churches lose contact and interest. I have talked with middle-aged people who worry about their parents in another city. They wonder about having their parents come to live with them—and ask me what to do. It is always dangerous to give advice, so I try to spell out the options. This is what churches could do.

The statistics about older Americans should challenge, not discourage, society and the churches. Creative new ministries by pastors and people are ahead. Many Americans have given up on the churches, but response to these new ministries could renew and energize congregational life —creating a social force to be compared only with the Protestant Reformation.

Congregations with large numbers of older members should not be considered to be "dying churches," contrary to the belief of many church people. They are indeed skill banks and reservoirs of rich, untapped, undervalued human resources and stimulating power desperately needed to renew and heal our sick society.

S: I think there are more possibilities for older adults than any other group, because they're looking for something worthwhile in which to invest their lives. There's a tremendous potential for the churches to work with this age group.

M: I'm glad you feel that way, because some ministers and congregations judge themselves to be failures if they are reaching only middle-aged and old people. I have heard them say: "I'm afraid our church is dying. We want to work with young people, not the elderly."

S: It's been my experience, though, that because of society's conditioning, people feel that when they reach a certain age, it's time to step down so that young people can come in. Yet age makes no difference in serving the Lord and humanity. It takes only one person who has a different perspective to set an example to the others—one person who does not believe life is over at sixty-five.

M: If you have people in your congregation or community group who have a mind-set of disengagement, how do you deal with that? Do you challenge it?

S: I don't think you have to challenge it. You can suggest or give feedback. In my church, people are coming to me soliciting responses, opinions, and advice. It's almost discomforting in some cases, because they're so willing. I want to say that I am not their age. Why lean so heavily on my advice? They're willing to take it, and it seems to be greatly appreciated, even though they may go out and do exactly as they please. But they do have a willingness to share with me. I don't get this same response from the younger members, many of whom are preoccupied with the rat race.

S: I have noticed that older people tend to be more dependent on other people for ideas, for reinforcement, etc.

M: What made them that way?

S: I think it's a problem of perspective. It's not that old people overnight magically transform and become dependent. It is the expectation of our society that by the time a person reaches old age he or she should need outside help. Because older people believe this, they put themselves into the role. The perspective needs to be changed.

M: It's hard to avoid the "doing *for."* Some people are hungry for attention and are quite ready to be cared for, well on the way to wrinkled babyhood.

S: I find that when persons are treated adult to adult, equal to equal, they move away from the paternalism or the infantile behavior.

M: But it is seductive. Many times you're hooked on a paternalistic stance before you really recognize it. I'm aware that some of us have believed the myth that old age is weakness and powerlessness. I can remember some of our members saying, "Hey, we don't do much *for* our 'older members.' " It is necessary to deal with immediate needs, which are pressing and acute and should be faced; but to make services the ultimate of ministry is to fall short of what could be for them and for you. Services should be provided to deal with the most obvious and acute need. If people are hungry and poorly nourished, then they must be fed. The delivery of a hot lunch to a homebound person may also be a way of discovering some basic health care needs, legal assistance problems, or housing complaints. It is probably a matter of multiple needs.

Much talk is going on in state and federal agencies about *home care.* What is being *done* is largely uncoordinated and quite inadequate. Churches could provide some precise "documentation of needs," which could be done without a big federal grant, and get competing groups together to serve the people. Homebound people should be crucial participants in the survey work and in determining what should be provided to enable people to remain in their homes.

One of the few resource books written for churches that are dealing with people in their congregation who are over sixty-five is Donald Clingan's *Aging Persons in the Community of Faith: A Guidebook for Churches and Synagogues on Ministry to, for, and with the Aging.* Don was on the staff of the National Interfaith Coalition on Aging and has done a lot of work with the Indiana Commission on Aging and the Aged. He is a Disciple minister. He wrote the *Guidebook* for the church's clergy and lay leaders. It gives specific advice about new forms of ministry, and offers statistical material documenting the challenge that confronts the church. It also deals with the interfaith aspect of ministry and suggests how the National Interfaith Coalition on Aging ought to be at work. He cites the objectives of the Interfaith Coalition:

1. To vitalize the role of the church and the synagogue in response to the new demography.
2. To give priority to the programs and services which meet the needs of older Americans.
3. To stimulate cooperatives and coordinate ecumenical efforts between the various major faiths in the United States and public institutions on aging funded by the Federal Government and by the states.

S: What are the limitations of this particular resource?

M: Clingan's book generally confines its scope to services and attempts to interpret the need for services without engaging in radical social change. There is a good section that cites the work that some churches have been doing to provide supportive services from their membership or from the community: Meals On Wheels, handyman chore services, friendly visiting to the isolated elderly, the transportation program which enables people to go to the doctor, shopping, and to church. There is also material that helps people work toward the advocacy role which certain churches should be taking in terms of the disadvantaged community. There's reference to legal problems of the elderly and a list of community resources that deal with legal problems of clergy, congregational ministry, retirement centers and nursing homes. The emphasis is on *service*. One would hope that beyond this guide there would be an emphasis that could be affirmed on removing the root causes for alienation, loneliness, and poverty—which, of course, is social change.

S: Maggie, what do you think of the Interfaith Coalition on Aging?

M: I am ambivalent about it. It has great potential, but at the present time it's not really off the ground nationally or locally. It seems to me that the Coalition is not daring enough; it's not moving in the right directions to really deal with these basic, root problems. It emphasizes service programs here and there that make people feel less pain and less anxiety, but the Coalition does not yet deal with the root causes of the anxiety or pain. Services are really novocaine shots, unless they sensitize people to the needs for social change.

S: It has been the desire of our congregation to become part of this organization, but we've been ambivalent about jumping into it. I understand that they try to organize networks by establishing clusters and a "Shepherds Center" program. From my perspective it's chiefly a social service network, which is O.K.; but if you stop there, it's an inoculation against social change.

M: That's a very perceptive comment about local in- terfaith groups that propose to deal with issues of aging. The Interfaith Coalition on Aging has no formal connec- tion with local efforts that may take a similar name. It is merely a national clearinghouse of denominations at this stage, and yet it could enable real advocacy for change.

S: How can we avoid dropping out because we're dis- satisfied with the ameliorative or pain-reducing approach? It seems as though we tend to stand aside if an organized program for old people is not good enough.

M: This is a hard question to answer, because time and energy are limited. If we feel that there is some hope in influencing the decision and getting in with our weight and insight to change an organization's policies, it may be a good use of our time. Grace Elliott, one of the early Gray Panthers, is the General Secretary Emeritus of the National Y.W.C.A. She is a distinguished social psychologist, now in her eigh- ties. She chaired the White House Conference on Aging section on Spiritual Life and Well-Being. She believes deeply that the Task Force on Spiritual Life, which operated in 1970–71, could be the seedbed for a new interfaith effort. The Interfaith Coalition on Aging was formed after that Con- ference adjourned. The Coalition received a substantial grant from the Administration on Aging of the Federal Gov- ernment to build this network and to enhance the role of the churches and synagogues—the religious communities of America—to accept new duties and to foster new kinds of religious-related activites. It is disappointing that the Coali- tion has not had stronger alliance with, and support by, social change advocates. Its potential for changing attitudes and moving in the direction of social change is yet to be realized.

S: I have a real problem with the fact that our congregation does not see the larger problem. Many of our people are willing to be involved and active. They have the means with which to exist and have a comfortable living in their old age, but they don't see the larger problem that you're so ably describing. In fact, they're part of the problem, if not the producers of it, who handed it over to their children who now keep it going just as Mom and Dad have set it up. I'm wondering how I'm going to show them that what they did was wrong, and maybe disturb their comfortable lives. They're willing to go on cruises and trips. They're willing to put up beach houses for the youth to enjoy, and they're willing to produce a facility that can house a day school for the children and do all sorts of things; but they don't want to disturb their comfortable *status quo.*

M: A few of those people, about 2 percent, can be aroused, if they're exposed. Maybe at this juncture you have to settle for the activation of the small percentage and let them create the excitement that will spread to a few others.

S: This matches my experience. Nine out of ten of the larger congregations surrounding us, with a greater percentage of the elderly, do not have a reputation for social action. When the Interfaith Coalition on Aging came into our county to organize, they pushed their blood banks program, which has really caught on like wildfire. But that doesn't excite our congregation, because there aren't that many people in our congregation who need blood. I find a built-in bias against doing social action, which is true of all age groups, but particularly true of old people. We have to settle for about 1 to 5 percent who will get energized and participate in the political and social processes of the community. My hunch is that that is why the Interfaith Coalition on Aging does not push social action. Their program doesn't try to get at root causes, and they cast too broad a net.

M: In our own ministry, even though a small number will actually be involved, faithfulness to the gospel requires some commitment on our part to enabling genuine social action to emerge. There are certain people who get a great deal of satisfaction out of helping others. They can build themselves a small empire around that helping service program and consider that that does the whole job. After all, they're working very hard, spending a lot of time and energy doing their service, and it's obviously needed; but it really doesn't change the system at any point.

A number of churches I know have set up car pools of volunteer drivers to take older members to shop, see the doctor, visit friends, and come to church. This transportation is a much-needed service, but the real issue is that we have woefully inadequate public transportation. Car pools meet immediate needs. They also take mass transit authorities off the hook. The Interfaith Coalition of your town might move into some important social action (beyond delivery of services!) to get public transportation for the elderly and the physically disabled. Minibus service, taxis with door-to-door service, dial-a-ride programs all are doable kinds of action that would benefit many more than local church members. In states like Pennsylvania and California the physically disabled have formed very effective advocacy groups. These groups would be natural allies in strategy to improve public transportation.

I'd like to see an Interfaith Coalition team up with the

disabled and start some dramatic action. All the volunteer riders should converge, with their carloads of elderly passengers and a lineup of wheelchair riders, to land on the doorstep of the state transportation office. Have a sit-in, following the ride-in, and press appropriate demands on the transportation bosses. It would be exciting and effective! Great for television cameras! Beyond *service*—ACTION FOR CHANGE!

S: Well, this has been our choice; but we have a very negligible number of winter visitors who participate in our ministry and a small percentage of persons over sixty years of age who will actually become involved. One of the things they sense when they come to our congregation is that we are asking for commitment and involvement. The ones we've managed to involve are really involved. They have a commitment to social change.

S: But is this happening at the expense of spiritual development? There's been a lot of reaching out and not much reaching in. It seems to me that we need to do a lot more thinking about the rhythm of the Christian life before the total reorientation that you're asking for is going to happen.

M: That's a pertinent comment, though I doubt that most congregations have been reaching out more than reaching in. The goal of those who have lived into old age is to be mature, developing, growing adults. Growth is spiritual. Where there is commitment to change and action, there is also some religious motivation, some spiritual growth going on.

II.
LIFE REVIEW

*Wisdom is found in the old,
and discretion comes with great age.*
Job 12:12, *The Jerusalem Bible*

M: Old people ought to have a sense of history. They must be encouraged to review their own history, valuing their origins and past experiences. With rapid technological change we are made to feel that our experience is useless. If we could stimulate a *life review,* we would see what we have lived through, the ways in which we have coped and survived, the changes we have seen—all of this is the history of the race. Older Americans have lived through more changes than any other human group. If we do not see the value of this experience because of our society's foolishness and our lack of insight as to what makes human beings really human, we will have done great damage to ourselves and to those who come after us. The churches, particularly local church leaders, have a tremendous opportunity to facilitate life review. Your ministries will be enriched and constantly refreshed by your being part of such historical processes. We can't turn back the clock, obviously; but I think that the church has an obligation to society, to the gospel, and to the Creator to assemble, across ecumenical boundaries, the accumulated experiences of the people in our congregations to solve human problems. I have a fantasy of skill banks where all kinds of knowledge could be deposited and drawn upon for the benefit of our ailing society.

On what events or experiences can this sense of history and the life-review process be focused? I've often thought it would be very interesting to talk about what people did to survive the Great Depression. It made great impact on all who survived it. The Depression and its privations and fears, the people's enormous capacity to face hardship, and the programs that President Roosevelt initiated can be reflected on in terms of social policy today. A lot of crass materialism grew out of the Depression years. We made a fetish of "things." The people who had so little got hung up on acquiring a lot. But there may be other kinds of memories and experiences that provide energy, creative power, and strength.

Life review can be helpful in a personal way, giving old people emotional reinforcement. By recalling past accomplishments and half-forgotten skills, memories can motivate and give new energy. Children love to hear about "the olden days"—it's a warm, pleasant kind of exchange and sharing that busy parents often don't have time for.

In the churches, by and large, we have emphasized (as public policy has) the weaknesses of age. We've catered to those weaknesses and tried to deal with them with a variety of social services, but we have not affirmed in any significant way the strengths of age. I have a feeling that our society needs those survivors and their experiences to give continuity and hope. There is so much of that wasted.

S: But there's also so much that seems to be deeply scarred. For instance, in Chicago the groups that have turned with the most violence and fear against the new groups that have come in have been ethnic groups. The stronger their ethnic identity, the more malicious their disdain for the newcomers. I can't find the redeeming thread in that history.

M: Maybe it was the expectancy—the Great Dream that many of these groups had initially of a new day, a new way. I think we're all questing and searching.

S: It seems to me that these are the unresolved questions that surface only when there is this great outside force, like the personal traumas in one's individual life that haven't been worked out. Somehow we need to find ways in which these wounds are brought to the surface and healed. We have the resources within us to do this. What do you do with some of this material? What is the follow-up? It can almost be another trivialization if you don't do anything with it or follow it long enough to let the benefits come forward.

M: I wonder to what extent the church, within its own congregational life, can demonstrate the pantomime of the gospel, in terms not of stepping on shoulders and pressing down lower groups, but in dealing with society in its present stratified form. There are great class differences. To what extent can the church, in her own life-style, demonstrate a cooperative/communal way of living—all things in common. Can affluent old people close ranks with the elderly poor?

S: I think the more pluralistic and diverse we can be naturally, the more we can model this type of community. Where we do not endorse societal norms that support class stratification, but we gather as a community, there is a oneness that transcends social stratification. Studies that have been done indicate that the more disadvantaged a family is, the more inclined they are not to participate in organized religion. In a way, this problem is similar to what we face with the aged.

M: People who have not been poor become poor when they're old. Cooperative life-styles, rather than competitive self-serving, might be developed in congregations. Cooperative housing and food co-ops could be organized and sponsored by churches.

S: Among the aged, there are not only those who are genuinely oppressed economically but others who have money in the bank but whose only income is their social security check. They are financially able to do something but they're going to nurse their savings.

S: But they also have their reasons. In our own county within the last two years, changes in the tax structure have quadrupled the percentage of tax that the low-income group pays—and that includes a lot of elderly. At the same time the amount of taxes that the high-income group is paying has increased only 5 or 10 percent. If they have a little bit In the bank, they have good reason to be scared.

S: And they still remember the Depression. They can remember the last ten years with inflation. Butler gives the example of a physician's widow who had $300,000 from her husband's estate and ended up on welfare before she died.

M: Maybe what you need to do, as a vocational group, is to perfect some skills in directing this life-review process. Nobody really has done this, that I'm aware of, within the context of pastoral theology and the exercise of this pastoral role. The possibility of helping people to really understand their own history is exciting.

In October 1976 I had the privilege of being a member of a study tour of the People's Republic of China. I was deeply impressed by the place of old people in the New China and what they are doing to "continue the revolution." They are teaching the children and the young people about the oppressive hardships and miseries of the old feudal order. They give talks in country schools, and share their grim and terrible experiences with university students. They work with the young and the middle-aged in Revolutionary Committees at all levels of government. Their remembrance of the past does indeed inform and energize the present. They are good teachers.

S: Roy Fairchild has prepared a little book that he calls *Life-Story Conversations.* He talks about "openers," "hookers," certain questions that will draw people out. He encourages a ministry of listening, in which all ages of people tell their story. This can be facilitated by trained visitors in local churches.

M: This is an interesting concept. It would be beneficial to have a small church, or clusters of people in a large church, do this. If those stories are shared and known, along with the skills that go into the making of a life history, the lives of all members will be enhanced. Churches could do this as part of anniversary celebrations.

In our consciousness-raising groups we've done something comparable, the rudiments of life review. It has been successful in large as well as small groups. We have begun with a *life line.* (See diagram.) At one end of the life line you put your birth year, writing it in large numerals (mine is 1905), not hiding it and not lying about it, because this is very important—this is the year your history began. On the

YOUR LIFE LINE

Jot down your earliest memories above the line: Your first Christmas, first day in school, first love, first kiss. First illness, first time hungry, first demonstration or protest, first petition you signed, first and most recent experience with violence. High school, college, your first job, first significant achievement, first failure, career changes. Marriage, children, first and most recent experience with death.

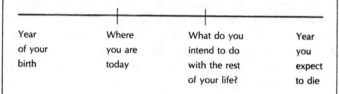

| Year of your birth | Where you are today | What do you intend to do with the rest of your life? | Year you expect to die |

Below the line note societal events in the community/world influencing your life: Strikes, violence, wars, epidemics, economic fluctuation. Technological changes in transportation, communication, industry, housing, neighborhood development and decline. Food habits. These jottings could be organized by decade.

In discussion trace interaction between personal experience and societal events and forces—how we learn to cope and survive.

other end of the spectrum, you put the year you think you're going to die. Whenever you do this, there's always a gasp. This is the first thing that helps raise people's consciousness of their own finitude, their own death. Mine is 1995. I would like to make it a little longer, but I don't think I will. Somewhere along the line, you put a notch where you are. Then there are two very important questions to ask: What have you done with your life so far? and What are you going to do with the rest of your life? Above the line you write down your earliest memories, which is another way of getting at the life review, the high points. These can be quite varied and exciting to share. Below the line you write your recollections of what was happening in the world outside you. You then get the interaction between your personal history and the societal history. The personal and the social are always joined, but we usually fail to make the connection. We also "lose" important social roots when we ignore life stories of older persons.

S: How long does it take to do that?

M: The time varies. It can be done in fifteen or twenty minutes as a starter for continued reflection that would go on at home. Groups can devote a two-hour session to some deeper probing, working first individually, then sharing in pairs or small teams. Some amazing memories have been recalled in groups where I have initiated the process. It is an easy way to spark general participation.

S: It's fun to write an epitaph too.

M: That's great. One of the choicest epitaphs I heard was written to Mary, beloved wife. "Here lies Mary, my beloved wife, under the only stone she ever left unturned."

S: Maggie, there are some other variations. I like that idea of putting on the life line what was going on in the world. It is a practical way to point out the church's social involvement. I've seen it done with high points of experience above, and low points, or traumatic experiences, below the line. Another way to do it is to have people draw their own line in whatever shape they want it to be, whatever metaphor they want. You use lots of colors. You don't write on it; you do it all in graphics. It's a marvelous validation.

M: Those could be displayed. There could be a rich interaction and exchange. There is a value in the graphic, to make feelings come out. People who are nonverbal can use graphics very effectively.

S: We had an interesting experience with the women of our church. Our women's groups have always been staffed by older members, and they decided they wanted to encourage the participation of younger ones. We had a friend come down who is a human relations trainer. She designed a whole day in which she led us through experiences that involved art expression—looking at a picture and writing down the words that came, putting colors to express the words, and then writing a poem from it. The women were so elated and communicative—they met each other on a completely different level.

S: One of the things that I started to do about a year and a half ago was to visit each member of the congregation on his or her birthday. I wanted to tie in to something more significant than just a visit. We had developed a plan of ministry designed around the three components: Study, Share, and Serve. I produced a little slip of paper with these components on it and tried to engage the person in dealing with his or her covenant with God and the church in those three areas. I found that that didn't work very well, because I didn't get that many slips back. I continued to visit with each person, however, on her or his birthday. I used a simple life-review instrument and centered the visit around "Let's talk about your life," which took it beyond the superficial level and yet was not demanding or threatening. They didn't want to reduce their commitments to a piece of paper that readily.

M: One of the things we found useful about focusing on each person's interaction with the world outside is that you help people to understand what they coped with and survived.

My generation has coped with fantastic change. I grew up in my grandmother's house, where there was no electricity. We had gaslight. My earliest recollection in public transportation was riding in a horsecar past my grandmother's house. It was like a streetcar, pulled on a track by a team of horses. In the summertime the horses wore sunbonnets. In the winter there was a foot of straw on the floor of the horsecar so your feet wouldn't freeze, because there was no heat. Now I experienced that myself. Last year I flew one hundred thousand miles in jets. Over a lifetime, all of that!

You can talk about the different kinds of energy, the changed life-styles, the pace, etc. You can reflect upon what was good about those other life-styles, what gave you personal and corporate strength to survive and cope with all those changes, how to calculate "the survival quotient" and depend upon your inner resources to see you through the changes that will come with age. If there could be a tapping of the hidden reserves and resources that the strong have, our society would be enriched and strengthened in many ways. How to do it in your church? I pose it to you, who have continuing access to people who have such strength and experience, to think through in your own relationships with them and to stimulate them to share their wisdom. If they're really going to be responsible and responsive to their own history, the sum total of what they are needs to be shared.

S: Are you familiar with a film by Ingmar Bergman called *Wild Strawberries*? It's about an elderly doctor who goes to get an award. He drives past his boyhood home. Then he goes to a community where he practiced. People still love him. He goes back in his memory, which takes him through his life. It's a very powerful film.

M: I've done life review with some of our Gray Panther groups. Some of our members come out of the Orthodox Jewish tradition. Many of them were born in Russia or Poland, and their earliest memories were of pogroms and harsh, terrible times of persecution in the ghetto. To have those people verbalize (and some of them can) about their childhood, their hopes and dreams of the New World, their experiences on Ellis Island, and then tell how some of those dreams were tarnished when they experienced the New World as it is today, is just unbelievably moving. It's a judgment. Many of them were Socialists. They still cling to their own Socialist tradition, even though some of them have become rich. Back in their subconscious, in their childhood memories and their early hopes for the new life in the New World, was the hope that there would be a much more egalitarian cooperative life-style, where everybody had a chance and where there could be relative freedom from fears—where everyone's basic needs would be met, not just the needs of a special, privileged few. Their experience is not only religious but it is also socially aware; so they could provide the motivation for some new politics. At present they are strong supporters for social protest and social justice.

S: There are many first-generation communities. One of the things that surfaced in our county in the Bicentennial celebration was the coalescence of some of those first-generation communities in a Bicentennial ethnic event. It was remarkably attended and celebrated with a great deal of pride. They're now working on a network of ethnic groups to continue the experience. They had an ethnic fair in the civic center, with booths and dances and singing.

M: But you see what we've done in America when we settled for the short-term goal? We created the melting pot. We taught the second generation to despise their roots. They were ashamed of their parents who spoke another language. They were ashamed of some of the old-world customs that came with the old folks. They neglected their language. We had a whole generation who knew not their history. Fortunately, where the Bicentennial took this turn, it made some reference in a prideful way to the deep diversities with which we've never dealt. This may be a dimension for your study, reflection, and life review with members of your congregation. It could be rich and exciting.

Life review is a method that stimulates social action, social analysis and protest—all essential for constructive social change.

III.

PLAYPENS AND WAREHOUSES: RETIREMENT COMMUNITIES AND HOMES

It is our want of passion, our inertia, that creates emptiness in old age.—Simone de Beauvoir, *The Coming of Age*

S: What parts of the Gray Panther action program on aging have been most controversial?

M: There are many problems in building a movement. Activists tend to hold strong opinions; to reach agreement on issues and strategies has never been easy. We work on a grass-roots basis and encourage local networks to respond to the problems they can tackle locally. Controversies have arisen over local strategies, and conflicts have flared with some established groups. Sometimes they have questioned our coming on the scene. We have had good press coverage for all we try to do, and that makes for contention with existing groups.

Local groups that are part of the National Council of Senior Citizens have tended to feel that they are doing all that needs to be done for the aged. Usually there can be some coalitional effort on legislation like tax relief, reduction of utility rates. We don't think "turf wars" help anybody. We want to avoid them if possible. They are a terrible waste of time and energy.

We have some controversy with state and area agencies

on aging that are government-supported. Some of our people are pretty outspoken in their criticism. In some instances we've challenged the way in which nutrition programs are set up and the lack of anything substantive in the Senior Centers programs. That gets us into a lot of hot water.

S: How are you received at Leisure Village, for example?

M: We're not particularly welcome at Leisure Village. People who have bought that concept generally do not want to be disturbed. The denominations have put large sums of money—billions of dollars if you add it all up—into age-segregated institutions. I think that churches have been acculturated to build and to take advantage of federal policy that provides the money under various amendments and titles of the U.S. Housing Act. I'm wondering if now is not the time for us to question that. In Philadelphia, as in many other large cities, public housing has become a disaster. The vacancy rate in public housing in Philadelphia is around 65 percent. Many of the buildings (even the most recently constructed ones) are uninhabitable because of vandalism or lack maintenance. They house an aggregate of people with many diverse problems.

S: Are you saying that all of the church-sponsored homes that we finance simply perpetuate ghettos of agism?

M: This is a big, fat question.

S: There's a Leisure City in Clearwater, Florida, called Top of the World, which is a prime example of age segregation. Everything, except for grocery stores, is self-contained. The residents have several golf courses and tennis courts. To meet ethnic needs, they have Mediterranean, Spanish, Contemporary, American, types of architecture so people can live in the style house they want. It's right in the middle of Clearwater; but it's a secluded community, self-contained with its own buses and its own guard. I'm sure this is typical of a lot of other Leisure Cities. It's a fabulous ghetto, giving the appearance of a cosmopolitan community.

S: With the help of federally guaranteed loans, major denominations have put a lot of money into programs of whole, self-contained units. The Westminster Project started in Indiana is moving across the country. It's a whole package deal. There are a wide variety of facilities—from high-rise apartment buildings, with infirmary and hospital facilities, to individually purchased cottages or condominiums. All these types of living accommodations are packaged within a geographical area. Every service needed is within the property.

M: My extreme categorization (and this really gets me into hot water!) is that they're playpens. They're very safe. Playpens are meant to be safe and comfortable. The people are out of the way of the rest of society. A group of gerontology students visited the Southern California Leisure World. Some went in with high expectations of finding paradise—Eden. One World they studied has ten thousand units. It's completely self-contained, with guards, a moat, barbedwire fences, a hospital, clinics, club rooms, even a community church. The students were concerned about the isolation, but they noted that some residents found it highly suitable and liked the life-style.

S: One of the social service agencies in our county that has an elderly-service component continues to report back to our board that the rate of psychological disintegration, suicide, alcoholism, and sexual promiscuity is disturbingly high in these areas.

M: It's gruesome. There's a facade of congeniality, but there is little real evidence of a true community. All of them have churches inside their boundaries. Yet they cannot seem to deal with the anxieties of their members.

S: What I hear locally is that in even the best convalescent homes people die and there's not even a note on the bulletin board. They just disappear. In one well-to-do place, when you get sick you must go to the convalescent unit. I can't believe this, but the people from the mobile unit are not allowed to visit because the directors think it would discourage them from going there.

M: In one place that I'm aware of, when people from the apartments get sick and are put in the hospital, they do not get visits from their neighbors. There's no prohibition against visiting, but there's apparently little motivation to do so. Many who are dying, or who have a crippling illness or a disability following a fall and who really could use some company, don't even have the comfort of friendly visits from the people with whom they've lived. I would hope that the church-related facilities would have as their goal the founding of a real community. The policy of building age-segregated communities and homes has to be challenged. Other options for residential living ought to be developed by the churches.

S: I've seen the other side of this whole picture. In Hawaii we have quite a few retirement centers. The striking thing is that they're filled with all Caucasians—no Orientals. There are a lot of isolated Asians who move into the homes of their children. Asians believe it is shameful to send older persons away to a home; but, in effect, when they move out of their neighborhoods, the older people become isolated from their friends. When they're really too old to live alone, they have to move away from communities in which they've lived all of their lives and go to live with their children in order to retain their sense of dignity. Many times their children resent having to care for them and only do it because it is their duty. The parents become demoralized and give up living. Isolated from former friends and familiar surroundings, they have nothing to look forward to. They die lonely—and their children are relieved. I wish we could promote retirement centers for Asians in Hawaii, because maybe even a facade of congeniality is better than this.

S: This suggests another problem that the church has to address somewhere along the line, viz, dying with dignity. To what extent is there real virtue in keeping the death rate down so terrifically low and fighting this dying process all the time, only to keep a person alive in a depressing environment?

M: I'm in total agreement with that. When we talk about health, I think we're really talking about death too. There can be health in death, or rather, a healthy attitude about a natural part of human existence.

S: So often we try to make our present and future out of the past. The WASP type of people who've gone through the Depression and want a nice safe place to be in their declining years opt for this playpen-type community because of what their past has been. Asians want the family image to stay intact, so they operate out of the past and also dehumanize the human experience.

M: Would the Asian historical norm be approximated if the extended family were set up not on the basis of kinship, but on the basis of some common caring? Can the local congregation become to some degree an extended family?

S: The problem with that is again part of this historical development. Because the young people have left many of the rural communities, I'm not sure they have adequate human resources within that geographical context. We don't have the mix we used to have in congregations to make it work.

M: In some churches we don't. Our social policies and present life-styles suggest that we ought to hold to the hope that congregations might change. We need to organize our neighborhoods in a way that encourages extended family life, neighborly interaction and support, and alternative living communities.

S: One of the original housing ventures was a United Presbyterian home in Washington that was simply an emergency type of setup. People bought a cottage situated on individual lots. The churches did provide this relationship. There was nothing there at all except a small infirmary and a dining room; otherwise you had to use the community. And there were two strong Presbyterian churches in that town that provided fellowship. Maybe that experiment of forty years ago was not far wrong.

M: What we're saying is that we're caught with an institutional arrangement that has to be looked at, critiqued, and analyzed for its values and its weaknesses. There's something to be done with church-related retirement and nursing homes—residents of those places cannot be abandoned. Though day-to-day skilled nursing care is necessary for some people, and some nursing homes offer excellent services, we must not continue to institutionalize people who should be enabled to stay in their own homes or in homes where they could share communal living with people who care for each other. All of us have to build our own parachutes, and intergenerational living may be one of them.

Meanwhile, I assume that any church that builds and operates an institution for older persons should have much higher standards of performance and excellence, and that a quality of life should pervade such institutions beyond what exists in the profit-centered residences. Now I don't know whether they are really that good, whether there's a discernible difference in our church-sponsored homes.

S: But does that effort to enhance the quality of life justify the kind of discrimination they perpetuate? So much of the church's values and dollars are locked into that type of age segregation.

M: There's no ease in Zion. I assume that all of you are in a very difficult position to raise some questions about the plans of the congregation, the conference, presbytery, district, or regional church body.

S: Allow me to share an experience in that regard. For five years I've been serving on the board of a retirement home called John Knox House, built in 1969 by the presbytery, which has a guaranteed loan from the Federal Government. It houses three hundred units for the poor elderly, and it's totally rent-subsidized. Soon after it was built the Nixon Administration cut off all funds for rent-subsidized housing for the elderly, so it's the only one in the area. Most of these people are paying about thirty-five dollars a month for their apartments.

Two years ago a colleague and I put together a resolution for the presbytery that would require representation of residents on the boards of all housing projects. (The presbytery has thirty-two hundred apartment units for the elderly under its ownership and management.) What happened to that resolution on the floor of the presbytery? We got clobbered with hard data which indicated that the kinds of tensions and internal anxieties associated with representation on the board of directors by the residents was more than they wanted or were willing to handle. If a resident becomes a member of the board of directors, then he or she becomes the focal point for the concerns, the complaints, and the anger of the members of the facility. When this came to a vote on the floor of the presbytery, we were voted down on the basis of hard data that had been solicited from the residents themselves. There are many complications in this whole question of self-determination. Within a highly defined residential facility the kinds of pressures that go with self-determination are sometimes more than the residents themselves want to cope with. What we ended up with was a compromise—in which there would be a residents' committee in every facility and every one of our boards would designate a member of the board of directors to sit on that residents' committee to serve as a bridge.

M: Isn't that interesting! I worked with a United Presbyterian General Assembly committee on a report that opened up the self-governing issue and advocated residents' councils and representation of residents on governing boards to correct some of the paternalism in church-related facilities. It became a controversial issue which the General Assembly committee could not resolve. It never got out of committee. The majority were convinced that old people do not want this responsibility. Have we raised a generation of people who are ill prepared to cope? We have not moved as church members in the direction of helping people take responsibility for their own lives.

S: That's why I like your strategy of working with the young. Until we raise people who want to self-govern from childhood to the grave, we're going to get a response that will frustrate our ecclesiastical commitments.

M: That's a very good way to put it.

S: Are you going to spend some time dealing with the alternatives?

M: Yes. We can explore these opportunities together. If we can get our denominations to make at least some investment of funds and commitment of leadership to new models, we might get a chance to give them a try before saying they won't work. Maybe some of you who are members of influential committees can raise the question of alternatives.

I would like to see some research that illumines the ultimate social consequences of separation, voluntary or otherwise, of the elders of the tribe from the young. Have you ever heard a group of old people say: "I hate kids. I don't want any young people around me. I don't like them"? What that does to the young and what that does to society is a very important ethical question that churches cannot avoid.

One of the models that the Jews have tried in Philadelphia, which I think is useful for a big city, is to build a high-rise apartment building with funds from affluent congregations. It is somewhat like John Knox House, since there's subsidized housing for elderly Jews who are poor. Then some people said, "Let's try something else." In another part of town, but not too far removed from the high-rise apartment building, the Jewish community has bought twenty-five old houses in a borderline area where Jews are moving out and blacks and Puerto Ricans are moving in. They have rented these houses to a mix of people, economically and age-wise. They have provided a skillful social worker to supervise and provide whatever services are needed. It has worked, and it has accomplished two things. It has provided alternatives to the large high-rise institution. Potentially each of the small houses can become a family. They can do things together (e.g., cooking, chores). Everybody has a bedroom and other private space, but there's also public space that they agree together to use jointly. They're very much concerned with the issue of faith, and they are served by a rabbi who has a large Jewish congregation in the area. But it would be interesting to raise the question of whether there could be a "house synagogue." There's a backup hospital and rehabilitation center, where people from that housing unit can go in case of an emergency, so that they're not moved too far from the living situation. The overall expenditure, the capital investment, in these living arrangements was much less than it would have been to build new facilities to house the same number of people at the present land values and housing construction costs. People pay rent, but it's according to their ability to pay.

S: *The National Observer* a few months ago had an article about homesteading in the inner city, in which houses were given, or sold at a low price, to people who would come and renovate them and occupy them. You add that concept to this one, assuming that the church could homestead, and there might be a real opportunity here.

M: Yes. The homesteading plan is intended to conserve neighborhoods. The Jewish experiment has helped to stabilize a large area. It's constituted a continuing anchor. The cities are in such deep trouble that, without those kinds of colonies, I hate to think what's going to happen. In Philadelphia there was a big housing project built by Stonorov, the famous architect, which was supposed to be an architectural wonder: twelve stories high. There were three buildings, housing two thousand families, all low-income. Elevators were immediately inoperable. There were few services provided to help people with mounting problems to live decently. In fewer than ten years, half of the apartments were uninhabitable and people moved out as quickly as they could. Now less than a third of those apartments can be lived in, so the Housing Authority is trying very hard to resettle those families. And guess whom they're going to put into that place—the old folks

IV.
HEALTH

Tho' much is taken, much abides; and tho'
We are not now that strength which in old days
Moved earth and heaven; that which we are, we are;
One equal temper of heroic hearts,
Made weak by time and fate, but strong in will
To strive, to seek, to find, and not to yield.

Alfred Lord Tennyson, *Ulysses*

M: Let's talk about health. We don't need to elaborate the health crisis: the shortage and expense of quality health care, the abominable distribution of it, its fragmentation and ultraspecialization—all converge at this particular period to make health a national issue, affecting not only the elderly but people of all ages. What we have is "sickness" care. We spend more for the treatment of disease than any other nation—close to 9 percent of the gross national product (which is well over a trillion dollars). We spend little for preventive care and often pay dearly in dollars and suffering for the treatment of the doctor-induced, or iatrogenic (*iatros,* "physician"; *genesis,* "origin") disease, which Ivan Illich probes in his book *Medical Nemesis:* "Iatrogenic disease comprises only illness which would not have come about unless sound and professionally recommended treatment had been applied." It is his most radical contribution to contemporary social thinking—and must reading to understand the nature of the American health empire, which is a highly profitable interlock of the AMA (American Medical Association), corporations that manufacture drugs and hospital equipment, and insurance companies. Ruth Mulvey

Harmer investigated the medical establishment. Her book *American Medical Avarice* (which is another way of spelling AMA) is another statement of the problem.

S: What about corrective legislation, like National Health Insurance?

M: A number of bills have been introduced in the Congress (at one time seventeen were floating in and out of committees), reflecting increasing public concern. The Kennedy-Corman Bill, which is an amended version of the earlier Kennedy-Griffith Bill, has had the most support. Many groups, including organized labor, have given staunch and unwavering support to that legislation. But I don't see it as the public policy to correct the excesses of the medical-industrial complex and its monopoly over health care. I see all the current bills as increasing the medicalization of life. A major exception is proposed legislation to create a National Health Organization, controlled by consumers, which delivers comprehensive health care and supplementary provided by salaried health workers and emphasizing health maintenance and the prevention of disease.

There is a good deal of evidence that the AMA is losing ground. Their membership is down about 50 percent and they're experiencing a slow erosion of power and prestige. The medical empire has been moving toward a new power base. The rising stars are the great medical teaching centers. They attract enormous federal research grants. They have been working with powerful private interests that have raised private money for hospital expansion and hospital buildings. The present situation is that we have overbuilt hospitals. We have centralized our medical personnel, resources, and facilities in key medical centers, which have gathered prestige, esteem, dollars, and power. Meanwhile patients are rarely seen in their homes, rural areas continue to be deprived of service, and the quality of care continues to decline. There's a good deal of evidence that the hospital era may have reached its zenith and is beginning a slow decline. One very important example is the number of hospital beds that are empty. We have overbuilt hospitals. We thought we had a good system for health planning, but we didn't. Instead of combining their resources and pooling personnel and equipment, hospitals have competed furiously with one another. Every hospital has to have its dialysis and cardiac equipment, the latest medical technology. The doctors' prestige depends on it, and powerful business interests go along. Hospital boards continue to be dominated by the doctors and two or three business executives. Patients' rights are rarely talked about, but malpractice is on everybody's mind. Medical education itself is highly competitive and dehumanizing. Young students may come in with idealism, but the system drains it out of them. They get caught in pressures to acquire quickly a large, lucrative practice where they think the dollars are going to flow. They have succumbed to another value system that makes it difficult for them, as human beings, to be human.

S: In the kind of world we live in I doubt that anyone is worth $150,000 to $200,000 a year, which is what some specialists earn.

M: Our third party payment system, with insurance carriers and Blue Cross–Blue Shield picking up the tab, acts as novocaine too. The patient doesn't feel the full pain of the high costs of service and hospital care, so there has not been sufficient public judgment on the real expense.

S: People who are concerned with moral values and with the quality of life ought to be thinking about the ethical questions involved in medical economics.

M: Let's summarize the issues here:

1. The maldistribution of personnel, resources, and equipment is getting worse. Forty percent of the public still lives in small towns and in scattered rural villages. Yet there are two hundred counties and thousands of small towns without any doctors whatsoever. Hardly any doctors practice in the inner cities anymore, except the Medicaid mills that have moved in on the medically indigent and are able to get direct payment for services from state welfare sources. The elderly, the minorities, and the low-income populations that are trapped in inner cities are most in need of good health care and have the highest incidence of illness. More than ever they are forced to seek care in the clinics of large hospital systems. These institutions have dehumanized the people who are connected with them: the hospital staff, maintenance workers and aides, as well as patients. The whole system is not a healthy, consoling, healing operation. Doctors who have been practicing in rural areas for many years went there as young physicians, stayed, and had a real commitment to that particular region. As they die or get too infirm to practice, they are not replaced.

2. Our health system is increasingly impersonal and mechanized. Young doctors are taught to read and to use the machines, but not to touch the body. They are taught to have more faith in those machines than in their own skill and manipulation. Of course, there are exceptions; but technology dehumanizes and removes the human touch.

3. The acute-care hospital is the model for the whole

health system. Providers of service seldom treat people where they live.

4. Care is highly specialized. Though there is some evidence that medical students are showing some interest in family medicine, little attention is focused on primary care and the concept of understanding patients as whole persons in their total life situations.

5. Peer review of the practice of medicine is often a cover-up for professional error and incompetence. Specialization and the lack of responsible peer review may be basic causes of the increase in malpractice suits and the rising cost of malpractice insurance. Malpractice insurance was a rarity and malpractice suits seldom occurred a couple of decades ago.

6. The discharge process is sloppily done. Technically the doctor is responsible for discharging the patient, but he or she is never around when the patient is actually discharged. Seldom is the information fully communicated as to what continuing care may be needed.

My brother died after being hospitalized for three months in three hospitals in Philadelphia recently. I was depressed and enraged by the way in which the whole health care system has been specialized. There was a succession of six different nurses who saw him. Each spent a few seconds—a couple of minutes at the most—but nobody looked at him as a whole person. In the top teaching hospital in Philadelphia he contracted a staphylococcus infection that ultimately killed him—and we did not even know until his autopsy that he had that. There was no primary nursing care, where one nurse looks at the whole case. It was the nurse's aides who had more continuous contact with him and who saw to it that he was looked after. How accurate can the reports be when each primary nurse is responsible for an incredible number of patients, with very little time to spend with each? The charge nurse who was supervising never came to visit him. The one person who was the kindest and most loving was a priest. He came to visit every day and was a friend to everyone—Catholic and non-Catholic. He was a beautiful guy.

S: What can we do about hospital calling?

M: I think that ministers have a unique role in this system. I would love to have you test out in your own ministry the elements of a new role that transcends what we usually call "hospital visitation." It is the role of the *patient advocate.* It would be a great role for retired clergy. If we validate this experiment and make a case for it, maybe we can get funding from a foundation or corporation to underwrite the training and development of patient advocates. They could become a new category for employment and an alternative to the mandatory retirement system. Churches should be motivating people to have more than one career. Pastoral skills should be transferable to other fields—ministry to doctors, to medical students, to nursing students, to the hospital workers. These service providers ought to be encouraged to function as teams, not pyramids of power topped by physicians. The patient advocate is not a novice. This is a person who goes into the clinics, emergency rooms, recovery rooms, and wards with tested experience, self-confidence, and knowledge of the system. A peer among peers. This transcends any routine hospital visit with a prayer and a little Scripture at the parishioner's bedside. Obviously this would take training. The dimension of it, how the training is set up, and who does the training is an interesting question. This is all conjecture at this moment, but I'm citing the reasons for it and some of the issues that indicate change is in order. There are all kinds of new frontiers!

S: If you know the law, there are doors open right now. All you've got to do is insist on your rights. If you've tried other avenues and they haven't panned out, insisting on one's rights can be the start of an advocacy program. Charts are not by law denied to ministers. In the states where I've lived the ministers have access to the delivery room, the recovery room, etc. The only place ministers cannot go is the operating room. Some of the places we assume are closed to us are not.

S: Does a retired person have the authority necessary to convince the hospital system to allow for this kind of program?

M: This we need to discuss. Otherwise we are continuing to scrap pile all the people who have experience who are not connected with any explicit job.

S: Gaining that necessary power base is really achieved by organizing.

M: That's a good point. I hope "visiting the sick and infirm" also includes visiting and advocacy in nursing homes. There are many extended-care facilities run by religious bodies. These nonprofit homes should be models. Often they are not.

While the media have called attention to the growing scandal of deplorable conditions in many American nursing homes, the first book to deal comprehensively and concretely with what *you* can do about it is Linda Horn and Elma Griesel's *Nursing Homes: A Citizens' Action Guide.*

Unlike many of today's complex social issues, nursing home reform is highly susceptible to local action, and Horn and Griesel pull no punches in telling you why, where, and how to apply pressure. No lasting reform will occur without consistent citizen monitoring and pressure.

The book provides a "tested strategy for change," based on the nursing home reform activities of local Gray Panther networks and many other citizen action groups all over the country. The authors provide a wealth of ideas by describing the innovative and successful projects now in action in other communities, from New York City to Lawrence, Kansas.

As an invaluable reference tool, the book is organized as a practical community action guide. The basic goals, organizing strategies, suggestions for interviewing, doing power structure research, and lobbying are all stated as direct and precise instructions.

Here also is one of the most accessible summaries of major legislation, literature and resources relating to long-term care, a problem that eventually touches almost every American family.

S: Look at all the hospitals supported by religious groups in this country. There we should be able to get some cooperation through the office of the chaplain. If we can't crack the other hospitals, at least we can start with those which have some religious ties. They're generally insensitive, too, to the same kinds of problems, because they've bought the system. They're part of the medical establishment. But through the influence of regional church organizations probably some sort of sanction could be obtained much more readily than in a community hospital. It might even be valuable to enlist their cooperation in the planning so they won't feel something is being done behind their backs.

S: What would the job entail?

M: As we see this job, the patient advocate is not an employee of the hospital. Nor is the role to be confused with the chaplaincy. The patient advocate should be working under the consumer protection agency of the state or as a volunteer under the aegis of the council of churches or the local or state interfaith coalition. If we do this testing effectively, the job should be set up ultimately by statute. In other words, what we are attempting in this interim is to validate the job and to see how it best can be carried out. We are also interested in seeing where it exerts leverage in the administrative structure of hospitals and how patient complaints and grievances can be most humanely and expeditiously handled. The patient advocate would conduct the following functions:

1. Interpret the Patients' Bill of Rights to the incoming patients.
2. Interpret the functions of the patient advocate to the patient and his or her family, so that the patient advocate is seen as a trusted ally and confidant.
3. Monitor the care of the patient, including the daily review of the patient's chart and interpretation of the chart to the patient.
4. Assist the patient in going to and from the treatment centers, operating room, recovery room, X-ray.
5. Assist the patient's family in understanding the nature of the care and treatment which is being received.
6. Receive complaints from the patient and his or her family.
7. Act as liaison between the medical personnel and the patient as needed.
8. Spend time with the patient in determining on a person-to-person basis his or her well-being and comfort.

9. Plan, with medical and nursing personnel, for the patient's discharge from the hospital, interpreting the follow-up treatment and medication that may be needed.
10. Visit the patient as needed, in the place of residence or the convalescent home.

In addition to the patient advocate, who works largely with individual patients on a one-to-one basis, we see the urgent need for a new role to be demonstrated for the *health care advocate,* who functions in the general field of health and monitors the local health care system. Newly enacted legislation has created health service agencies. They are to oversee and approve the allocation of funds for health facilities, the location and building of hospitals, the purchase and acquisition of hospital equipment, etc. This requires a sophisticated kind of consumer advocacy which we see the health care advocate monitoring. Federal guidelines call for a majority of consumers to serve on all health planning bodies, including the health service agency boards and advisory committees. There should be health care advocates also working in clinics, laboratories, and local health care facilities such as nursing homes, as well as on Blue Cross–Blue Shield boards. In the monitoring role we see the following functions:

1. Collection of consumer-oriented data on health problems and gaps in service. Ideas from interested consumers and suggestions for the resolution of problems could be included in the data.

2. The establishment of communication between health providers and consumers: doctors, nurses, visiting nurses, health agencies, private agencies, public health authorities, sanitation engineers—all who are concerned with health.

3. The monitoring of the handling of complaints, including public complaints and taking action to resolve them. Complaints requiring regulative action should be appropri-

ately referred. But there should be some follow-up to see whether the appropriate bodies to which they were referred actually do anything about the complaints.

4. Serving as patients' rights advocates in institutions, assuring enforcement of the rights of patients, promoting understanding, and monitoring for accountability.

5. Organizing and conducting referral systems regarding health services and the adequacy and availability of state and federal programs.

We see health care advocates as important in assisting in the planning and developing of new home health care systems that would care for people in their homes and in the neighborhoods where they live. We're very much interested in having churches take a more active role in health planning and considering this a legitimate part of their outreach. Health care advocates would work with the press, television, and radio. They would publicize health issues and problems, develop greater public awareness, and generate deeper community concern. They would attend meetings of health agencies to start communication between agencies and the individual professionals (social workers, health educators, scientists, nutritionists, etc.). Here the church could play a pivotal role in bringing these people together. In many congregations there are nurses, doctors, nutritionists, health educators, who could be supported in their larger responsibilities to the public, as well as to particular patients.

In Philadelphia we have begun a small grass-roots experiment in neighborhood organization which we call The Health Block. Its goal is to achieve maximum mental, physical, and environmental health for a particular census tract with a large percentage of older residents. There will be teams of *health builders* (old and young residents) who will be responsible for assessing neighbors' needs for health care, and alerting a team of *service providers* to serve residents in their homes. The teams will work from a neighborhood *good health center,* which focuses on health maintenance. Special attention will be given to environmental safety, including safety of the homes and streets, and elimination of such health hazards as vacant, vandalized houses and trash-filled vacant lots. Each team of health builders will have special training. The service providers will work as a team coordinated by a retired public health nurse. An advisory committee representing the established agencies will evaluate the project. A social work student has begun initial neighborhood organizing.

The church could be active in promoting cooperatives reforming the health system. Churches can work together, by denominations or in ecumenical groups, to develop and provide training programs for citizens interested in becoming health care advocates. They could acquaint them with the intricacies of regulations in preparing them to testify in public hearings and to represent public interest in local politics.

Church members also have a very special role as consumer protectionists in overseeing and watchdogging the sale of hearing aids, eyeglasses, drugs, and dentures to assure proper care at fair prices. The sale of hearing aids is a lucrative business. Church members should be educated about how to buy such devices and where to look for proper help. The whistle should be blown on hearing-aid dealers who exploit the hearing-impaired. Standards should be developed for the sale of hearing aids and the protection of people who are suffering hearing loss.

What we need to do is to approach this advocacy project as a team effort—and not put ourselves on the top of a hierarchy. This also would require lots of communication between ministers to foster a sense of a community of support to function in what can sometimes be a "lonely profession'' and to promote mutual spiritual growth.

The American Hospital Association several years ago adopted in principle a Bill of Rights for Patients. But there was no mandate with it that hospitals had to interpret the Bill of Rights to patients. It was there, and if you knew it existed, you could use it as your guide. A couple of Gray Panthers in Cincinnati, Ohio, took on the cheerful duty of going to every hospital and asking where the Bill of Rights for Patients was displayed, who interpreted it, and how it was used in admissions procedures. They raised quite a lot of fuss and got it displayed. It takes that kind of gutsy persistence to make hospitals, their patients, and the whole staff aware that this document exists. Various legislative efforts have been made to require hospitals to display and interpret it. The ministerial association could make that a target operation.

Decisions about health services that are going to be provided for a particular community are often made in secret, without really good public exploration of the services and their availability, or documentation of the need. There should be a community-wide group that would really zero in on the need for health care, develop a bill of particulars, and show where there is neglect, shortage or absence of care and service. They should be watching the health service agencies. Maybe then some changes could be made. Congregations could have a health planning task force that becomes knowledgeable and helpful in dealing with the new health service agencies that are coming down the pike and are going to repeat the same errors as in the past. Some advice along this line is available in Michael Dowling's book, *Health Care in the Church*.

V.

MANDATORY RETIREMENT

The meaning or lack of meaning that old age takes on in any given society puts that whole society to the test.
—Simone de Beauvoir, *The Coming of Age*

M: More than four thousand Americans reach the age of sixty-five each day. They are not discernibly older, either physically or mentally, than they were the day before. But sociologists note that they have moved into a new category —the aged. From that day on, they will be treated as "old" by the government and by employers.

On that magical birthday they lose one of their most important legal protections—the age discrimination law, which protects workers between forty and sixty-five.

Paul Woodring, in the *Saturday Review* of August 7, 1976, writes: "Because Congress has decided that it is legitimate for employers to discriminate against employees *over* sixty-five, they can be discharged without a hearing regardless of their health, vigor, intelligence or alertness. It is not called 'firing'—we use the euphemism 'mandatory retirement.' " The result is the same: employees have lost their right to continue to do the jobs they know best; and, what is even worse, they face perhaps twenty years of unemployment.

The Gray Panthers have chosen mandatory retirement as their special legislative issue. The elimination of mandatory retirement is the target, and the hope is that existing age discrimination legislation can be amended to make it illegal to discriminate against people on the basis of age at any age. We believe that mandatory retirement is a socially wasteful and often personally devastating social policy. Retirement should be flexible and optional. Mandatory retirement has to be challenged and changed for the following reasons:

1. It is a form of discrimination based solely on age.

2. It forces many older persons who would prefer to continue in their work into earlier retirement. In other words, it prevents full-time or part-time work from being a viable option.

3. Mandatory retirement removes needed skills, energy, and involvement from the labor force.

4. It forces many people to live on greatly reduced and fixed incomes, usually half the income they received while working. In this reduced-income status many people are forced to accept a life of poverty and dependency.

5. Forced retirement damages self-esteem and hurts many people both physically and psychologically.

6. It affects working people of all ages. For example, it is increasingly difficult for a person in his or her early forties or fifties to change jobs or careers. They're often considered "too old."

7. Mandatory retirement perpetuates negative stereotypes about aging (i.e., old people are not productive and should spend their time in leisure activities; they can no longer compete with people in younger age brackets).

8. By perpetuating negative stereotypes, mandatory retirement diminishes the humanity of all of us. Children and young and middle-aged adults are socialized into these attitudes. Old people often internalize these myths of uselessness and behave accordingly.

9. It creates artificial barriers between age groupings. We

lose continuity with the person we are and the person we were and are becoming.

10. Mandatory retirement is a mistaken remedy for an economy which is unable to provide full and meaningful employment for all who are willing and able to work.

11. Mandatory retirement is an outgrowth of social values that favor competition, efficiency, and energy capital–intensive production, instead of maintaining an ecological balance and releasing the potential of human creativity in the work environment.

S: There are some strong arguments for mandatory retirement. Some people want to get away from hard and stressful jobs.

M: Mandatory retirement has often been described as a policy designed to allow older people to reap the benefit of their work by spending their final years in leisure pursuits. Some people do look forward to a vacation, but not a vacation for the rest of their lives. A Harris poll shows that 86 percent of Americans believe that people should be allowed to continue working if they can perform effectively. Mandatory retirement is represented as a kindly and efficient way of removing the less capable and less trained workers from the labor force. However, this assumes that older workers are less capable than younger workers, and that it is not worth providing workers of all ages with training opportunities and chances to upgrade their skills or to move into jobs in which there would be more adaptability and rapport.

Powerful and vested interests oppose changing to flexible and optional policies. The administrators of large organizations (both public and private) and organized labor are concerned with the supposed lack of efficiency. They firmly believe that their older workers are more prone to pitfalls of the Peter Principle. They also believe the myth that they have lower production rates and are no longer able to compete with younger workers. Mandatory retirement is seen as an effective means of eliminating inefficient workers, especially in public jobs where civil service regulations provide greater shelter for inefficient employees. Labor opposes any change in retirement policies, partly from its desire to expand and not constrict the job market and to provide openings for younger workers in the job market. A long-range educational campaign is needed to build a base of understanding of the need for legislative change and also for experimenting with the way in which acquired skills can be transferred to second and third careers in the worker's later years.

S: There is nothing wrong with enjoying leisure at all ages, but why is it necessary to force leisure on people? Doesn't mandatory retirement violate the individual's right to work and the equal protection clause of the Constitution?

M: Civil liberties groups agree that forced retirement does indeed violate the individual's right to work and to equal protection. They further agree that the elderly are a special class that warrants special target legislation to offset age discrimination to which they are subject. They are a "suspect class," a judicial term that means "subject to repeated legal oppression such as affect racial minorities."

A brief look at the history of retirement-related policies may also help to answer such questions. In 1890 workers over sixty-five made up 68 percent of the labor force. In 1960 they were only 30.5 percent. (These figures are from Clague, Palli, and Kramer.) In seventy years we moved from a predominantly rural, agricultural economy to an urban technological economy. Agricultural work was just as strenuous as most work in the 1970's. The high participation of persons over sixty-five in the 1890's labor force points out that productivity does not come to an end at some fixed age.

Between 1890 and 1970 there was a great increase in the productive output per work hour. Fewer people produced much more. This resulted in shorter work weeks and was also partially responsible for the institution of mandatory retirement. The Depression of the 1930's led to the demand for more work and income-maintenance programs. The establishment of the Social Security system, with its retirement test, served the function of enticing many people out of the labor force in return for generally inadequate income support. World War II resulted in a greatly increased demand for workers; and, during the war, social security benefits were kept at very low levels. In part this served the function of enticing older workers back into the labor force, including a number of women who returned to work. Since World War II, there have been significant, though not really sufficient, increases in social security benefits. Elaborate pension-retirement systems have developed. Unions have usually favored retirement policies that move out older workers, and these policies and contracts have been negotiated to put workers out at increasingly earlier ages. These factors, among others, are the supporting cobwebs of the policy of mandatory retirement. However, the American Medical Association has opposed forced retirement and offers empirical evidence of the negative physiological and psychological effects on retired persons.

S: Mandatory retirement serves the needs of an economy that is unable to provide employment for all those who want to work. Let us really face this fact and recognize the need for reordering our national values and priorities in order to provide jobs for people.

M: The maintenance of an institution that forces older people out of their work roles requires perpetutation of an agist belief system. This system requires that all groups buy into the concept that old people are less able than young and ought to enjoy leisure time, even if they don't want it.

S: As the deceptive nature of this concept is recognized, more attention will be focused on the important social question: Why is the economy unable to provide full and meaningful employment for all who wish to work?

M: That is a fundamental question, an ethical question that churches should be raising.

Social Security was enacted in 1935. Its goal was to provide a supplemental income that would be linked with individual savings or jobs. The necessity of it was clearly evidenced in the Great Depression. Retirement rates have been responsive to economy figures and have mirrored the upswings and slowdowns in the economy, rather than basic changes in individual attitudes toward work and retirement. In the 1930's few people were eligible for social security; agricultural, household workers, and the self-employed were all excluded. Through the years benefits were extended to other categories of workers, until at the present time nearly all working Americans are eligible for social security benefits. In the 1940's came the beginning of pension plans. These were linked to full employment, and they encouraged older workers to leave the labor force when employment opportunities declined. During the 1950's and 1960's, when our economy was expanding, social security pension benefits also were expanded and liberalized. Part-time jobs were possible. In the 1970's we see the phenomenon of increased forced retirement at increasingly earlier ages. It is shocking to contemplate that, even in academic

circles, college and university faculty members are subject
to the arbitrary retirement rule.

S: How well have present age discrimination laws protected our people?

M: In 1967 the Age Discrimination in Employment Act
was signed into law. It provided protection for those who
are at least forty but less than sixty-five years of age, but gave
no protection to persons over sixty-five. It was even difficult
for people under sixty-five and over forty to prove that they
had been ousted from their jobs on the basis of age. Other
reasons were often used to justify the separation of these
older workers from their jobs. There was no way to force
compliance unless workers were willing to complain—and
relatively few workers have been willing to do so.

S: Employees have probably felt that they can't do much
to change this policy. They try to make the best of a "bad
rap."

M: Union leaders have generally favored mandatory retirement and have usually excluded retired members from
union participation. Their argument is that their interests
aren't the same and that only the people who are actually
on payrolls ought to vote in union affairs. Many retired
unionists resent this and feel deeply that present union leadership has forced them from a prophetic role that was present in the union movement in earlier decades. Local unions
hope that their retired members will not be too visible. They
may give them a beer "bust" once a year, an occasional trip
through the plant, or a picnic. That's about the extent of their
contact with those who worked hard and who helped to
build the union.

Senior citizens' organizations have shown some interest in legislation and lobbying for arbitrary retirement amendments. The National Council of Senior Citizens, related as it is to the labor movement and including in its ranks large numbers of former trade unionists, has generally (until very recently) favored the arbitrary retirement rule. They believed that this was the only way in which younger workers could be brought into the labor force.

A great deal of time has been spent researching the physical effects of old age, but not much attention has been given to the question of arbitrary retirement. Gray Panthers support national efforts to institute flexible retirement policies; but in this period of high unemployment, it will not be easy to change policy without lots of pressure from voters. Not enough legislators have heard from their constituents. Gray Panthers have sent questionnaires to all members of Congress asking for their opinions. Responses to date indicate opposition to mandatory retirement.

Emphasis should be given to programs of worker retraining, recycling, and reclassification, which would improve morale and productivity at all levels. When I was doing a television interview for a Los Angeles station, the sound man handling heavy portable equipment was listening intently to our conversation about eliminating mandatory retirement. After the interview, he followed me down the hall, presumably to tell me privately how much he agreed. Then he lowered his voice and said: "You know, I'm going to be seventy-five in August. The station thinks I am going to be sixty-five. I have been working for close to thirty years in radio and television. I've been the sound man for a news crew for more than twenty years. I've gone to fires, scrambled up and down hills, and carried packs of camera and sound equipment that weigh close to a hundred pounds. I'm just as able to do that today as I ever was, and I have no intention of giving up. In fact, I don't know what I'll do if they force me to retire; but I'm not going to admit how old I am. That just goes to show how silly that rule is. Here I am seventy-five years old, lugging around stuff that they think I couldn't carry if I was sixty-five." He commended us for our work to end mandatory retirement. I asked him to support us when legislation came to a vote.

S: The people who have created retirement policies on a mandatory basis aren't often subject to them. Politicians, industrialists, and labor leaders like George Meany do not fall under their own axes. Can the Gray Panthers generate local pressure to convince local legislators and representatives in state legislatures and Congress that arbitrary retirement must be changed?

M: There are two legal arguments against mandatory retirement based on violations of the due process clause of the Fifth and Fourteenth Amendments. They are technical but important. Mandatory retirement policies violate "procedural due process" when mandatory retirement legislation deprives a person of an important interest (employment), without providing opportunity for a hearing. In the *Board of Regents* v. *Roth,* the Court indicated that when dismissal from government employment (as in retirement) would substantially interfere with the person's ability to secure other employment, the person is entitled to a prior hearing on the reasons for the dismissal to determine the validity of the dismissal. In several cases plaintiffs have argued that mandatory retirement statutes are unconstitutional under the due process clause, because they contain an unjustifiable, rebuttable assumption that all workers over a certain age are incompetent. By forcing workers to retire without individualized determination of competence, mandatory retirement statutes burden the right to earn a living, which has been traditionally protected under the due process clause. If the courts would narrowly construe the retirement benefits plan's exception under the 1967 Age Discrimination in Employment Act and expand the act to its proper scope to abolish arbitrary age discrimination in employment, lawsuits may become successful for public and private employees under this. The intent of the law is clearly to protect workers. Obviously the Supreme Court and other courts have yet to recognize older workers and their right to work, or to face the fact that they deserve greater Constitutional protection than they now enjoy.

The Gray Panthers are, in the light of these findings, focusing their attention on college campuses, as well as churches and judicatories, enlisting them to work for the formation of coalitions in support of changing existing policies. The challenge effort could well begin with the boards of trustees of institutions of higher learning and with church-related colleges and schools. Church-related colleges have a particular opportunity and responsibility to move in the direction of flexible retirement of employees of all categories: in administration, teaching, and maintenance. We plan, in our legislative strategy, to introduce legislation, state by state, to build support through our Gray Panther networks, educational programs, and speakers' bureaus. We want also to get the word out in our Gray Panther meetings and in the handling of the many complaints that come to our offices. We're encouraging all of the action networks to note instances of forced retirement that either violate the existing age discrimination laws or document cases of compulsory retirement at the age of sixty-five and over. We can work these cases through our task force and ultimately press class action suits on behalf of the workers who have been separated from their jobs.

S: What more can churches do?

M: Churches can help by encouraging older members to complain when they are forced out of their jobs. Ministers can send us reports from their counseling with members who have been the victims of age discrimination. We have been experimenting in the Gray Panther movement with new categories of jobs older Americans can do which make use of their skills. The churches should be sensitive to the retirement issue, encourage people to talk about retirement policies which they are forced to follow, and take appropriate measures to bring people together who have been facing similar problems.

The church should give more consideration to preparation for retirement. "Retirement preparation" in business and industry is shallow. It deals principally with retirement income and leisure time. Some retirement planners stress volunteer activities and hobbies. Again, they tend to trivialize age. The people who are packaging these retirement preparation plans are enterprising, and corporations are buying them for a lot of money. Churches should be challenging the waste of experience and skill. What society now presents is *accommodation to* the policy. The churches should be changing it.

S: I recommend a study guide called *Shifting Gears.* I think it's ineffective to hand people books; but, if you use this book with a group that's willing to sit down and really concentrate on the exercises, it could be a valuable tool. I think some of the seminaries are working on materials that are good; but we do need much more.

M: One book that I think is quite good, *The Retirement Book,* by Joan Adler, has specific and helpful personal advice; but few retirement books go beyond the preliminaries and deal with the inner journey that people are finding toilsome, the anxiety and boredom of unending leisure and rest that does not renew or revitalize.

VI.
CHANGING LIFE-STYLES

Many are the miseries of an old man
Who seeks a fortune and fears to use it,
Who seeks the future and fears to lose it,
Who lacks courage, spirit, fire.

Horace, *Ars Poetica*

M: Education in the churches that leads to action and moti-vates social change is difficult. But it's part of the empower-ment of people who are deprived of their power by their lack of place in society. It really can't be neglected. I like to think of the church as the motivating force to encourage old people to go back to school. The continuing education movement is a tremendously vitalizing and empowering force. There are community colleges all across the country, which offer exciting courses. We all have access to new knowledge, and new knowledge refurbishes the mind and the spirit. The church can set the pattern and the example. You might possibly consider having a course, or an offering of courses, in your church that would be extension courses from the community college, places that are not too accessi-ble for people in outlying areas. Our church buildings could be much more widely used for such purposes. With that kind of service and opportunity for learning available in the church, maybe people would be enticed to go back to school.

In some instances, particularly with blue-collar people, it's extremely difficult to motivate them to go back to school.

Learning evokes unhappy memories for many of them. You could help them see that their own life experience equips them to learn extraordinarily well, if they would just believe in themselves. I had a poignant experience last year in northern Wisconsin. I was asked to do a two-day seminar by the Sociology Department of the University of Wisconsin at its Marshfield campus. At the end of the two days, I was invited to speak at the regular meeting of the Marshfield Senior Citizens. They were meeting in a most unattractive hall, a barnlike place just across from a beautiful college campus. The Sociology Department was terribly concerned because there were no old people enrolled in any of their courses, and they wanted to know why! So they sent me over to see if I could stir up any interest. I talked about the college, and the interesting classes offered without charge. I said: "Let's just take over one of these classrooms right now. What are you doing sitting in this cold, barny place? It's most uncomfortable. Let's go over there; they want us." But my arousal didn't do a thing. They just sat there. After my speech ended, they were clustering around for coffee and doughnuts. When nearly everybody had left, two old men came up and told me that they were the oldest people in Marshfield (ninety-six and ninety-eight) and they would like to go to that college. They hadn't even finished grammar school. They'd worked all their lives in the northern woods as lumberjacks, but they said that they knew a lot about history.

"We're history buffs. We like history. We sure would like to take one of those history courses."

I said, "You ought to be teaching one of those history courses over there."

"Aw," they said. "We couldn't go over."

"Why couldn't you?" I asked. "They want you."

"Think of what the neighbors would say," they answered.

"What are those old fools going back to school for? Looking after those pretty girls?"

It would have been a nice idea, but they could not bring themselves to do it. Apparently the social pressure of this town and the social pressure of their peers were so extreme that they couldn't take advantage of something that they really wanted to do. Think of what they would have done in a history class! The motivation to continue to learn is not easy. But in the context of the church, maybe you could get around the mind-sets and discover ways to motivate. The goal of successful aging is to keep on growing and learning and becoming a mature, responsible adult.

S: Let's make sure that whatever centers start are not exclusively for the old. There should be a mixing of the ages.

S: That's a good idea, but sometimes difficult. I think this is something that the church has to resolve. We do have available a community of people that is cross-generational, but young people have their own objectives. In our campus ministry, we have a program designed for those fifty-five and older, but open to everyone. We don't have many younger people involved, but at least they're welcome. We encourage the older people to take credit courses at half tuition, and an increasing number take the credit courses after they've become accustomed to being on campus.

M: We're so accustomed to tracking people by age that it takes extra effort and imagination and a really radical critique of all of that. Cameron Hall, in defining adulthood, says that there are three stages of personhood. There is childhood. Everybody knows what childhood is. We're just beginning to hear about the rights of children. There's a big debate about when adulthood begins. Is it when you can drive a car, get your license, legally take a drink, get a marriage license, vote? That's not a settled question, but Cameron Hall says you can be very sure that adulthood has ended and the third age has begun when people say to you, "Oh, how marvelous you look!" It's very interesting to watch that.

Another educational task is to equip us "old folks" for new roles. I feel that old people have a particular responsibility in our society to develop, test, and try on for size some new roles. The roles are patterned after the model of the elders of the tribe, who are responsible for the tribe's survival and for those who come after. There is absolutely no excuse for any of us to retreat to our own private worlds because of our age. There are all kinds of reasons why we do—why there is alienation and anomie and all kinds of rejection of others and turning inward.

We the elders should be society's futurists. We ought to be doing future testing of new instruments, new technologies, concepts, ideas, and styles of living. We have the freedom to do so and—we have nothing to lose. There are increasing numbers of people in my generation who are equipped and who are ready to do that, if given an opportunity. Not a large number, but some. They would like to swim against the tide of fierce economic competition and try other kinds of arrangements whereby work gets done and common tasks are shared—cooperative living; communal use of property; barter; exchange of skills rather than money; instead of fee for services, exchange for services. Putting together a skill bank in a particular congregation might facilitate that. Who knows, out of such modest, small experiments some new knowledge and economic systems might emerge.

S: In reference to co-op living, there's quite a wide range of possibilities. An example is food co-ops. A group could be responsible for buying cooperatively in bulk, the storage of food and its disbursement. I see this as a real possibility for retired people.

M: It's a socializing force too. It helps people work together to establish some new interaction with one another. Also, it certainly is an alternative to food marketing by agribusiness. Instead of having these nutrition sites where they just give people food, I think they ought to be staging areas for organizing food cooperatives and monitoring harmful additives. I wish we could get these into the federal guidelines, so that they would be part of the operation of Title VII nutrition programs. There ought to be much more gardening, yet so many places are built without any kind of access to land. We should also think of the possibility of community gardens on our church property and open spaces around church-related homes. The facilities that we now own, control, and have access to should be used in a new way. If we're going to build new homes, let them be co-ops. Let us support a new kind of economics. We ought to be watchdogs of public bodies—guarding the public interest in township meetings and planning boards, particularly on the boards and advisory committees that deal with government programs serving old people. The guidelines for programs of the Administration on Aging call for 51 percent of the constituents to be members of the governing boards. But they're token old folks. They don't know too much about what is going on and they just sit there. They ought to be alive and interested and equipped to assume their role as elders.

S: I want to back up a minute to make a point about these working cooperatives—maybe gardening, or working on cooperatives in condominiums. One of the things we find in our church is a desire on the part of older men to participate in hard work. Some fellows are almost feeble, and yet they like to go out and paint. If they want to paint for a couple of hours and then rest, that's all right with me. Some of them can't get up on ladders, but some of them can. You could spread the work out so that everybody takes a piece of it, and you end up with a team. I stress the voluntary nature of my project. They work a couple of hours whenever they think they can and do their best with it. Most of the time they can go farther than they think. But I don't ask them for a full, eight-hour day with the pressure that we so often think has to go into our American-type economics. It's an easy approach to the work.

M: It also demonstrates, perhaps, a new kind of economics. There could be team-shared jobs, even by younger workers. Again, we're programmed. But in our old age we're free to try new things, we're free to innovate, we're free to burst out of old wrinkled skins and be creative. It takes some planning to do that. It takes a few examples. And it takes our own confidence that this is possible. I wish that some of you would really look at your congregation. If you have affluent oldsters, see if you could do something together. Think of how they could raise some very important questions in the next stockholders' meeting. Instead of just sending in their proxies, they could be there. They could raise questions about mandatory retirement and corporate policy, and environmental protection issues, depending on what the corporation is. Some older stockholders could get more involved. If they are free from the eternal drive to get the highest dollar yield on their stock, they could press for corporate responsibility and accountability to the larger public good.

I like to think that we could release, in our time and in appropriate ways under the aegis of the church, healing agents. I'm enormously struck with what antibodies in the human body do to combat disease and put down infection. I'd like to think of us releasing healers—people out of their own understanding, their own sense of history, their own freedom from some of the tyrannies of earlier years—to help heal a sick society in whatever way they can.

Another responsibility of the church is to counsel adult children. We need to bring together adult children who are anxious, antagonistic, and hostile about their relationships with their parents. There's a lot of pain and guilt which we've glossed over. We've just assumed that families are going to get along, but they don't. There's enmity and discord. We've got to find other living arrangements. In some instances maybe it isn't good for adult children and their parents to live together. We could assemble, and assist in developing, extended family arrangements that are not based on kinship—mixes of people who have a common goal, who have some commonalities and who can indeed become an extended family. I think of the congregation as an absolutely marvelous place to let that emerge. The adult children need much counseling about their parents' sex lives. It's a touchy topic. If one spouse dies, and the other spouse has an opportunity to remarry or have a love affair, all hell breaks loose. It causes great tensions. There ought to be rejoicing rather than such hostility. The wise counseling that is offered, and the kind of prevailing ethos that is set by the formal leaders of the congregation, can begin to shape a new climate of dialogue and acceptance.

S: My wife manages an office with a half dozen women working in it. One of them was a widow in her fifties. She was going to get married, and it was a good match as far as we could see. But the three children were just up in arms. It was almost as if she were committing adultery.

S: The real problem is the guilt this creates, which sometimes doesn't even come to the surface.

M: It has to be worked on and worked through. You can help it to come up to the surface—or you can gloss over it.

S: Sometimes your opportunity to talk is with the married couple. They can be helped to understand that their children or the rest of their family probably will be upset. They can then meet the resistance and quite often work through it with their families, as long as they're not caught off guard.

M: You can fortify them, and give them the strength and support they need. Perhaps they can do it a bit more easily, if they're assured that you think it's all right.

S: I would also try to talk to the children, just to help them understand that this is an acceptable situation.

M: The children may have some faulty sex ideas too. Their own sex lives may be pretty messed up. There's a lot going on that we need to examine in a wise way. If you're doing this, you ought to read Butler and Lewis' book on sex and age, because it gives some good physiology and knowledge about the sexual competencies of old age. The book is called *Sex After Sixty*. It's simply written. You could lend it to a couple to read, and also lend it to the children. It's a dimension of sex education that we've long neglected. Most marriage counseling doesn't get into this at all. I've participated in a symposium on Sex and Age sponsored by the Philadelphia Marriage Council. SIECUS (Sex Information & Education Council of the U.S.), under the leadership of Dr. Mary Calderone, is providing excellent materials and guidelines. Old people should know that sex therapy is available.

The churches should be particularly concerned about the kind of counseling that is done on the sex problems of old people. Ministers do have many opportunities to meet with young people as they contemplate marriage and establish themselves with mates. They often counsel people who are facing divorce and dissolution of marriage. But there's been little attention, either in the marriage counseling agencies or in the churches, to the sexual needs and the human sexuality of people who are in their later years. It's assumed that sex is a no-no—that sexual competence, interest, and the ability to attract members of the opposite sex are lost when one gets old. Such mythology must be eliminated from the thinking of people and from the practice of society. Institutions under the direction and guidance of the church frequently violate the humaneness of the situation. Spouses are often separated by institutions and housed in separate rooms, deprived of the kind of comfort and closeness which could be so important in their daily lives. Attendants violate the privacy of residents by opening doors without knocking. There ought to be a lot more openness in discussions with the adult children of older men and women. Adult children should be helped to see that their parents need to have companionship and love, and that there is nothing strange about interest in marriage or sex or even contemplating a love affair. Affection ought to be encouraged rather than decried and discouraged.

We haven't even talked about the older woman. I believe that the older woman really needs the liberation message. The thought of close love relationships between women is also something with which the church ought to be coming to grips. Many churches have experienced a great deal of controversy over homosexuality as a general subject; but in a large population of older people, where women so greatly outnumber men, lesbian relationships may occur to assuage the loneliness of old age.

Old women have few opportunities for sex partners among the opposite sex, unless they accept the attentions of younger lovers. This, too, is an option for the older woman and should be encouraged and understood, not criticized as it has been in the past. There's been little or no criticism of older men who take younger wives or have affairs with younger women, but it somehow seems perfectly awful for older women to have any connections with younger men. This mind-set has to be changed, and we are taking steps in our movement to remedy it. We hope that opportunities will be open to people of both sexes to establish deep friendships and loving relationships until *rigor mortis* sets in.

S: You're especially talking about the widow, aren't you?

M: I'm talking about the widow, and I'm also talking about the older woman whose marriage is still intact. Older women have much to gain by participating in the women's movement. Many will be widowed in later years and should find new selfhood and liberation from fears of loneliness by associating with younger feminists. NOW (National Organization for Women) has a Task Force on Older Women which is actively combating age and sex discrimination, especially in employment. NOW has stimulated the introduction of the Displaced Homemakers Bill, which would enable older women to enter the labor force and to use the many skills acquired in homemaking. Women's associations in churches have a crucial role to play in educating and counseling older women regarding their options.

Aging makes a big difference in many marriages. A couple who have lived together for fifty years with busy daily schedules have not had to confront each other on a twenty-four-hour basis every day. Each has had his or her interests. Their children are now gone, so there isn't that to hold them together. Maybe they have to move to a new place and change their living arrangements. Now they've only got each other, for better or for worse—and it's often for worse. They've not really worked out a solid marriage. In their old age they've got to, if they're not going to kill each other. A churchwoman whom I once knew well called me one day and said: "I can't talk to anyone else, Maggie; but I'm going to talk to you for about an hour. I'm just going to tell you that I'm leaving my husband. We're having our fiftieth anniversary—and the day after that, I'm leaving him."

"Why?"

"Well," she said. "All of the time we were married, I had responsibility for the home and the children; and after the children were gone, I did a lot of things in the women's program of the church. I've also done some enjoyable things in the community on various boards. My husband thinks that I ought to give up all that outside activity and stay home and take care of him—that my community and church work were to keep me entertained only while he was away. But those responsibilities meant something to me, and I can't give them up. Since my husband retired we've had such tension and hostility that we're both sick." I asked her if she had talked with her minister.

She said, "I can't talk to him."

I said: "Why don't you try? Maybe he would understand."

"Well," she said, "I'm ashamed. It seems as though we ought to have worked it out, but we haven't."

I won't go any farther with the story, but I just want to say that hers is not an isolated case.

S: I've seen an example of this tension between older couples in the grocery store where I shop. The wife will pick up something and put it in the cart and the husband will say, "We don't need that." Sometimes he'll take it back out of the cart and put it on the shelf. My judgment is that probably through their lifetime she has done the grocery shopping—and now he's taken over her role.

M: That's a beautiful illustration of role reversal. Her role continues, but they both have to find appropriate roles. It's a very real problem, and the tension can mount.

S: Perhaps it could be a positive opportunity for the wife to relinquish some household tasks that she'd rather not be responsible for, if both she and her husband were in agreement. This is where counseling could play a useful role.

M: Yes. What about the possibility of setting up a speakers' bureau? You might encourage some of the lay people of your church to make themselves available. You and they might fan out across the country or the county, spreading a different concept about old age. Some could lead workshops. Some could give lectures on sex or on death and dying. The new word about the third age needs to be carried far and wide.

A real missionary territory, if there ever was one, is the nutrition site. Title VII, of the Older Americans Act, provides for congregate feeding. Most of those places are feed bags or soup kitchens. But they have the possibility of being educative and socializing. Much more could be done with them. If you had a battery of speakers who wouldn't mind taking on that burden, it could be marvelous. Eating is a ceremony, a celebration. It's symbolic: Breaking of the Bread. And there ought to be meaningful words exchanged during a meal.

S: I got burned at one of those nutrition sites, Maggie. I was dancing with some folks down there. As I started to leave, this old man, who must have been about seventy, followed me out of the door. His face was rigid and angry. He started pointing his finger at me and said, "You know, my minister told me that when a man dances with someone else's wife, he has evil thoughts."

I said, "Sounds like your minister has a problem."

M: Oh, that's marvelous! There are so many possibilities to provide enlightenment and stimulus and to spread the word in a new way. You and your lay people have the ingenuity and the brains to communicate shared experiences. I spoke to a congregate feeding group in Southern California. When I got out, I just burst into tears because I was so upset by the sadness of that whole operation. This was a government-sponsored, government-funded nutrition site. It was a big one; there must have been about three hundred people there. It was the hardest thing I've done all year. It was absolutely distressing. The people were depressed and defeated. The stance, the way they looked, the way they walked, and their body language so evidently reflected depression and rejection.

S: From what you're saying, just having a dynamic speaker is not going to solve the problem.

M: No, it isn't. But, taking this on as missionary territory, maybe a couple of your older parishioners could start the healing process by acting as antibodies.

S: We're talking about exuberance and enthusiasm, and how you maintain it. Well, some people never get it. It wasn't programmed in us. Ralph Will, Sr., who was involved in church work in Central American and India, retired to Georgia and moved into our community. I've never seen a person like him. He began to grow roses. He went back to school. He became a leader of the speakers' bureau. He took his roses to everybody in the community. He visited every new person in our church. The young couples loved him. He learned to play the organ. How much of this is taught and how much is inborn?

S: One mental health study concludes that people who start out in life with this kind of initiative don't lose it. If they have always been withdrawn, introverted, or rigid, it's un-likely to change when they reach maturity—they're going to keep operating that way.
I was wondering if the kind of institution which you said seemed so depressing doesn't draw less self-generating persons to it. Maybe the ones who really have initiative and are self-enabling would be out somewhere else.

M: I think all of you ought to visit one of these nutrition centers just once to see for yourselves. Maybe you can't do much. Maybe it is not possible to heal, to reconstruct, or to revitalize. But for your own understanding you should send yourself on a little field trip just to see. In terms of responsi-ble social criticism, I have very mixed feelings about all those nutrition programs. People are hungry and are in need and many are living on pitifully small incomes. But the programs are reaching very few people. A crucial ethical question and an important public issue remains. How do we deal with that whole segment of the population: 23,000,000 people?

S: If society expected more from its older members, more enabling would occur. This is one of the conclusions drawn from hospital work with the mentally ill—and it includes the aging. When the administrators get in there and expect something from them, people will do more.

M: Many of the people who run those centers think of these people as wrinkled babies and treat them paternalistically. They don't expect that they're going to do much—and they don't. Changing the attitude of the administrators, and becoming acquainted with staff of the agencies on aging, would be good things for you to do. Through enabling work, lay people can influence public policy and institutional practice by observing, watching, monitoring, and advocating.

We who are older have enormous freedom to speak out, and equally great responsibility to take the risks that are needed to heal and humanize our sick society. I repeat what I said before: we can try new things and take on entirely new roles—dangerous roles. Let me describe some of them:

1. *Testers of new life-style.* In old age we don't have to compete. But we need desperately to cooperate, to live communally, to reach out to other human beings we never knew before. Our society worships bigness, numbers, profits. We esteem smallness, small groups caring for one another, small groups of activists taking on the giants. Small is beautiful.

2. *Builders of new coalitions.* Age is a universalizing factor, enabling us to close ranks among young and old, black and white, rich and poor—coalitions of power and

shared humanity, old and handicapped—natural allies.

3. *Watchdogs of public bodies—guardians of the public interest and the common good.* Cadres of watchdogs can observe the courts, watch city councils, and monitor the public and quasi-public bodies where critical decisions are made, often hidden from public view.

4. *Advocates of consumers' rights and whistle blowers on fraud, corruption, and poor services.* We need patient advocates in nursing homes, advocates of the hearing-impaired, advocates of elderly residents in retirement homes.

5. *Monitors of corporate power and responsibility.* We can establish media watchers to monitor television and the press. We can organize protests in stockholders' meetings, reminding the multinational corporations of the ultimate ethical questions about their operations, safety of their workers, protection of the environment, etc.

6. *Healers of a sick society.* We can use our weakness and deprivations as powerful social criticism and levers for change.

7. *Critical analysts of contemporary society and planners for its future directions—shrewdly assessing our materialism and the ersatz values of our plastic world!* Life-styles of outrage and activism predispose toward quite new roles for the professionals working with us. There is much that we need and must do together. In this age of liberation and self-determination, ministers, directors of homes for the aged, coordinators and directors of the federal, state, and area-wide programs for the aged, doctors, nurses, social workers, counselors, and educators have to shift gears. They must stop treating us like children and wrinkled babies. There is massive paternalism for us to overcome. Well-meaning professionals doing for us simply have to be challenged.

You are performing well in the public interest when you are enablers, energizers, liberators. Many of you are caught in bureaucracies which hold you captive and which you can't change. We can be your advocates. We are outsiders, you are insiders. Together we can change things. Things are not going to be better for any of us until some basic societal changes are effected for all. We are talking about more than what old people want for themselves. As I put it in a paper published by the University of Southern California:

> [We] have worked through and gone beyond the so-called "Senior Power" view of ourselves and the way we want to use our experience and years of accumulated skills and knowledge. We do not wear *Senior Power* buttons or think of ourselves as special pleaders for the cause of old people and old people's campaigns. . . . Our goal is to use our freedom, our experience, our knowledge of the past, our ability to cope and survive, not just for free bus fares or tax rebates for people over 65, although we need these benefits. We want to work as *advocates* for the larger public good, as public citizens and responsible consumers. (Paul A. Kerschner, ed., *Advocacy and Age: Issues, Experiences, Strategies,* p. 89.)

VII.

THE CHURCH'S CONTINUING ROLE WITH THE AGING

The ethical possibilities of life are broader than any philosopher has guessed, stronger than any psychologist has suspected.—David Hackett Fischer, *Growing Old in America*

M: Churches and synagogues have a tremendous opportunity in the last years of this century for creative new ministries, if they take seriously the experiences, skills, and human resources represented in the older members of their congregations. The churches are acculturated like other institutions in Western society and still remain youth-oriented. I believe that this is a detriment to their ministry. It deprives the young of a holistic approach to life as a continuum; and if the churches are still oriented to the youth, they are either neglectful or highly paternalistic in their attitudes toward older people. But agism works both ways. It's very cruel for the young, people in their late teens and early twenties; it's very oppressive for people in their later years. There are many commonalities that the old and the young share, only society has kept us apart so we seldom have an opportunity to discuss or even consider how much we have in common.

How shall we deal with aging in our present society? What are appropriate responses by the church? There are ten points which I'll briefly describe. Together they comprise the continuing role of the church.

1. *The educational-nurturing role.* Churches transmit the tenets of our Christian faith to the young, the middle-aged, and the elderly. Christian education and nurture ought to be a continuum, just as life itself is. Christian nurture, as I see it, ought to deal in a very substantive way with attitudinal change so that people in their middle and later years understand themselves and have built into their own self-images a sturdy approach to the kind of demeaning, diminishing attitude that society takes toward the human aging process.

The church has not paid enough attention to spiritual-intellectual nurture of older people. To begin, the church library should have pertinent books and periodicals for older persons as suggested in the Bibliography.

At the same time we need to plan more significant educational experiences with older persons. Our children and young people are presumably in church school classes or on retreats, so they are participating in a formal program of Christian education. Christian nurture is supposed to be an ongoing task of the church, one of its unique characteristics and vocations. It may be that the insights we're getting about age today, because we're confronted with the new statistics and the facts of longevity, may help us to refine and extend the whole process of education to enhance the quality of life in the community.

E: I'm aware of a tremendous tendency in most churches to single out the elderly—in Christian education and in most social services.

M: Church education is age-segregated. Education in the churches and in public schools is age-graded education. Educational materials are written for children of various ages, young people, and adults. It really separates people by age. Perhaps this approach to Christian education should be questioned and serious consideration given to integenerational learning. A few churches have been experimenting with education which is not entirely age-segregated, which enables old people to contribute to the nurture of the young, and which enables young people to prepare themselves for new roles. The old should be interpreting their experience as a part of the educational process. Would it be feasible to institute special Sundays or church family nights when there could be some intergenerational or cross-generational teaching and learning? I can imagine some younger teen-agers spending an hour or so Sunday morning or evening with the oldest members of the congregation, recording their conversations on portable tape recorders and playing back the tapes for more general discussion/education (e.g., using life-review procedures described in Chapter II). The Christian education committee could work out some good lively questions for starters.

I saw some fascinating experiments in a Lutheran congregation in Philadelphia where most of the members were old and white. They were scared to death of the big black teen-agers who had moved into their old neighborhood. There had been some purse-snatching too. The young pastor teamed up with the social studies teacher in the high school where the teen-agers were enrolled and designed the interviews as a class project. Gray Panthers assisted in bringing teen-agers and old people together. It was great all around. Fears and tensions lessened. Trust was built. New aspects of the gospel were clearly shown. They established interaction and built some trust. I don't know how far any follow-up went.

E: What might they have done to make this learning more action-oriented?

M: They might have worked out some kind of escort service whereby the black teen-agers would take the elderly shopping and be their protectors, instead of their attackers. The Black Panthers, in their early stages in many of the large metropolitan areas where there were Black Panther activities, included a very successful escort service. The young black men would offer "safe passage" to older people in the ghetto. I understand that a group now beginning to work in Philadelphia has money from the Law Enforcement Assistance Administration to fight crime on the streets. They're doing it with a rather thorough community organization effort, pairing up people who need protection with the people who might otherwise have been their attackers, giving young people who need money some small remuneration, and also training people to have more pride in their community.

2. *The counseling role.* Many pastors have had clinical training in pastoral counseling. They have been extremely helpful in dealing with the problems and crises of their parishioners. Their counsel is trusted and appreciated. But we see that the counselor's role needs to be augmented by the counseling that educated, concerned, and informed lay people can do, particularly in training and counseling for the retirement years.

E: Have you seen any efforts by churches to train their own people to do this?

M: I haven't to date, and this is probably because I haven't been traveling as widely as I should and observing as many churches. I would hope that for the near future this would be a goal. Even though people have worked hard and have looked forward to their retirement, when their retirement day comes, following the "gold watch" ceremony, there is a great trauma—and some people never recover from that shock. There is anxiety and fear and a very great loss of self-esteem.

E: It would be refreshing to imagine a congregation actually dealing with these fears, letting people talk about them. I suppose it's much easier to gloss over the problems and assume that retirement is "wonderful."

M: That's a very good comment. This is how most congregations probably would treat it, despite the fact that people go through more psychological changes in the last twenty years of their life than they do in the first sixty. Older persons experience the traumas of retirement; death of friends, spouse, children; lack of income, health, mobility.

E: Is there a special reluctance on the part of old people to seek pastoral counseling on this subject, or any other?

M: Some of the people whom we've been in touch with, who have called us, or whom I've met in my travels have said that they are pretty sure that their ministers would not understand. They're loath to bring those problems to the attention of their pastors, and this is sad. They probably feel somehow that the ministers are too busy or too preoccupied with other administrative matters to take the time to talk with them.

E: How are pastors going to obtain this special sensitivity, since they have not experienced retirement?

M: The pastors could indeed enlist the help of lay people in the congregation who are going through the shock and are quite upset by it.

E: One technique a pastor might use is to gather recent retirees to talk about what they've been through in order to educate him or her. In the process the minister might convince them that they ought to do something with other people who are retiring.

M: Yes. They themselves could serve as a resource for counseling and all kinds of very practical advice for people who are preparing for retirement. The preparation should begin in middle life. Church members in middle life don't want to think about getting old. They are too preoccupied with getting ahead and keeping ahead in the rat race. But when there is a crisis in their lives, or with their aging parents, they look to the church to help in some way. When they are compelled to retire from their jobs, they often retire from life. I think we have to lay that all out in front of our congregations and do what we can to help them to see other options.

I think that the church has another task in its counseling role—education in human sexuality. Sometimes that doesn't come into the counseling setting, or there are questions about it that members of congregations hesitate to ask; but ministers should feel comfortable enough with that whole field of human life to bring up the question if it isn't brought up by the counselee. There's some technical information which needs to be sought by the laity and ministers about social security benefits and some of the complications that exist in getting those benefits and pension rights worked out. Sometimes employers will give you that advice, but they may not; and the church ought then to be counseling people to what they really can expect.

E: Do you picture this as including primarily the members, or some kind of community service? Oftentimes the church is surrounded by older people, especially in transitional neighborhoods, who do not necessarily belong to that congregation.

M: I would hope that the counseling role of the church would be extended to the community and that the pastor and other people in the congregation would seek out, in a changing community, some of the isolated old people, because they are really shut out from the usual services that are available.

3. *The congregation as an extended caring family.* We think of the church as ministering to and involving in its membership the conjugal, or nuclear, family—fathers, mothers, and children—but in the church family there are people who don't particularly fit that formula. I'd like to think of the congregation itself as being an extended family, including people of different ages.

A few years ago, Hoekendijk, the Dutch theologian, was talking about "the pantomime of the gospel"—the acting out of the gospel message of love of neighbor. The church's own life-style could indeed be made to demonstrate ways to order and reorder the structures of society. The church can provide some models for society. For example, the church has structured much of its own life and worship in terms of the family—the conjugal, nuclear family consisting of father (the breadwinner), mother (the homemaker), and young children needing the care and protection of parents.

Increasing numbers of church members don't fit that family mold. They are quite apt to be widows, divorced parents, adult children living far away from parents, etc. Our mobile postindustrial society has put great strain on nuclear families and practically destroyed the old extended family. I'd like to see congregations become extended families, providing mutual assistance and emotional support for their members— extended families not based on kinship but on common concern. Children who seldom see their grandparents would have associations with old people. In turn, lonely old people would have some young ones to look after. The congregation, as an extended family, has an opportunity on a continuing basis to care for its members and to provide the kind of support that families usually provide. There could be shared tasks. There could be care of members who become ill or disabled, or face the crisis of death or accident.

I'm wondering whether the deacons, or a similar group, could be given major responsibility. In the Presbyterian church deacons have a duty to visit the shut-ins and care for "the poor" of the parish. It seems to me that the deacons could take on concern and advocacy for older members who are lonely, infirm, and homebound. Many of these people may indeed be poor and living on shockingly low incomes. Social service agencies employ outreach workers to do what deacons and other lay people in the churches should consider as a mandate of the gospel. Deacons should make it their business to find out what services are available and see that necessary services are provided. Meals On Wheels and homemaking and nursing services are available in many communities. Deacons should be monitoring such services and pressing for their improvement. Church leaders have clout that we often fail to use. Compassion is not enough. Friendly visits are obviously the first steps in establishing and maintaining contact and finding out what the homebound really need. Some of the deacons might take training and then function as counselors.

E: How do you reach that stage where people really care for each other in congregations?

M: It's probably an advanced stage of congregational life. Maybe it's wishful thinking at this point. I think, though, that a congregation could begin to try it in particular neighborhoods. Some churches have divided their membership into parish units. There is an effort being made to bring together people who live within geographical proximity of one another. Those people might look at who they are, what their particular interests and needs are, and begin to act like an extended family and move toward some substantial effort, rather than just a romantic notion. One kind of sharing which has become very popular is between older members of the congregation and young children of young families who haven't older relatives to help out. That could be extended. People have helped each other in times of bereavement. They've taken over the business of providing food for the bereaved family, for the relatives that may come. They house the relatives.

E: What do they pay the pastor to do then?

M: That's a tricky question. The pastor is the enabler, the organizer, the energizer for the new life-style; and that keeps him or her quite busy.

4. *Preaching the gospel. Proclaiming the word.* The teaching elder shares this task with lay people who also preach and speak. I think of preaching as extending into

something like a speakers' bureau, which could include pastors and lay people who go out to a variety of community groups and talk about the facts of growing old in a new, affirming way. Certainly what the minister says from the pulpit on Sunday morning sets the prevailing ethos of the congregation.

E: One practice that I've noticed in some congregations is that for a particular Sunday the preacher arranges some sort of preliminary study with a few people. They will actually look at the text or pick a text together and talk about its meaning. Maybe that would work especially well with some of the concerns that older people face. Why not study texts that pertain to those concerns and build a sermon together? (E.g., Ex. 20:12; Job 12:12; Ps. 71:9, 18; Prov. 21:29; Isa. 40:28–31; II Cor. 4:16; I Tim. 5:1–2.)

M: I like that. That's great. Another variation would be to have the minister announce this and then have some follow-up discussion in a coffee hour after the service to relate it to their particular living situation. The interaction of the congregation with the task of preaching is a great idea. I think of preaching as being informed by a thorough understanding of the Bible and also of the ethical-moral issues involved and the judgment that could be proclaimed in the Word. I think of preaching as not accommodating members to the faith, but of challenging the members to continue to contribute, to be socially responsible adults.

E: We don't realize how much we influence people by what we say. They can pick up on the tiniest point we make in a sermon. If we imply that somebody, because they're getting older, isn't quite as sharp, they will pick up on that, even though we're saying just the opposite in our little study group.

M: It seems to me that the effectiveness of preaching is dependent upon the whole life of the congregation. The church teaches by what it does. Preaching that is congruent with the whole life of the congregation does have a central role; but where real participation, goal-setting, and decision-making are lacking in the life of the congregation, where there is a lack of genuine affirmation of life and of each other in the life of the congregation, preaching itself won't make much difference. Preaching is effective within the context of a caring community.

5. *The social witness role.* This is another continuing responsibility of the congregation. The church can help to change the agist attitudes and policies of our country. Social criticism and analysis of our sick society ought to be a very important aspect of social witness and action. If churches took seriously the predicament of the young and the old in our age-segregated society and used their own channels of interpretation, communication, and interaction to discover the particular problems of the members of the congregation, the social witness of the church as a whole could be addressed to today's problems and the resolution of these problems.

Many people are very anxious about their elderly relatives who may become confused, or fall and have an accident, or develop some disorder or chronic disease with which they cannot cope. The housing needs of older people are very complicated; and I would hope that the church, which has met housing needs by building retirement homes, would look beyond that institution to the plight of old people in declining neighborhoods and would motivate its members to think of sharing housing space. Many widows who live in big, old houses all by themselves—and the majority of older women are widows—should be encouraged to share that housing space with people of other ages. This could be a beneficial experience for everyone involved. Since 96 percent of older persons live in the community, rather than in institutions, attention must be focused on noninstitutional housing and related needs.

The need for continuing citizen action to reform nursing homes and other extended-care facilities ought to be heavily laid on the conscience of the church. The United Presbyterian Women gave the Gray Panthers a grant to develop an action guide for citizens' groups (Elma Griesel and Linda Horn, *Citizens' Action Guide: Nursing Home Reform*); and we hope that many congregations will be using that material, investigating the nursing homes in their community, and working with nursing home administrators, staff, and patients to reform the system.

E: One of the frustrations that people probably feel regarding social witness, in terms of the issues facing older persons, is to get a picture of the key organizations and legislation. Do you have any advice to local church task forces on aging? How do they keep track of what's happening? Are there certain agencies at the city or county level that they ought to be particularly alert to, and what legislative handles do they have? Are there certain organizations that help them keep track of new legislation?

M: The field is burgeoning. There are state and area-wide agencies established by the Older Americans Act of 1965 and its various amendments. The Older Americans Act provides funds for state programs on aging and area planning agencies to coordinate services in the larger metropolitan areas and in the counties. The church should be familiar with staff persons in those agencies. From your State Commission on Aging or Office on Aging can be secured the names and addresses of the area offices on aging. The area offices do general planning and coordinating of what is being done for old people within a particular geographical area. The focus is on services. The church should be aware at every point of existing services—what they provide, what they don't provide, and how they can be secured.

There are three very large national organizations which have been organized with many local groups. One of these, the American Association of Retired Persons (AARP), and its sister organization, the American Association of Retired Teachers (AART), have more than 10,000,000 members across the United States and 2,000 to 3,000 local chapters.

E: Do they lobby?

M: They lobby on the national level very successfully for services and programs that will benefit the elderly. They're primarily concerned with "direct services" for old people. They're not too much into basic social change. The local groups tend to be social and recreational. The AARP provides an insurance program which Colonial Penn underwrites. It's a large and very lucrative insurance program. It provides different kinds of health policies that supplement Medicare and Medicaid and give reimbursements for extended hospital visits. There is a drug service, where people can secure pharmaceuticals and prescription drugs at reduced prices. There is also a travel agency that many people use which provides interesting tours. AARP publishes a magazine, *Modern Maturity,* and monthly newsletters.

E: If those large organizations spend most of their energy on practical needs of retired people (probably those with a reasonable amount of money who can afford insurance and travel), who is monitoring what the agencies do at the county level?

M: This monitoring role is something that the Gray Panthers have taken on. As you know, the Gray Panthers are a coalition of old and young people working for social change.

E: Do the Gray Panthers exist all over the country?

M: No, we have a limited number of affiliates: approximately forty across the country. We're stronger on the West Coast (especially California) and in the Northeast than we are in other sections. Or national office is in Philadelphia. There's a second structure, called the National Council on Aging, that has been working, in training and research, providing bibliographical materials and program resources. It has local councils. The third big group organized on a national basis is the National Council of Senior Citizens (NCSC). This, too, has local councils. It's closely affiliated with the labor movement, and the local groups frequently include retired union members who come into local councils for social activities. The NCSC provides health insurance coverage for its members and newsletters carrying legislative information at local, state, and federal levels.

E: Are they lobbying hard on certain issues like mandatory retirement, etc.?

M: They're lobbying hard for equitable and increased social security benefits. They've been highly critical of Medicare and Medicaid. They have not, until very recently, done anything about mandatory retirement. The unions have held the line on mandatory retirement. They have, by and large, encouraged early retirement and have negotiated union contracts on that basis. We feel that the time has come to challenge that, and Chapter V on mandatory retirement suggests why. All those groups are doing some good things, and the church should know about their general goals. In addition to knowing about the government agencies and these private, large agencies, it's important for churches to be on the mailing lists of state offices on aging so that they can be aware of state and local legislation that needs to be supported. They should also be on the mailing lists of the Senate Special Committee on Aging in Washington and the House of Representatives Select Committee on Aging. Those committees have been doing investigative reporting, have conducted hearings in Washington and across the country, and have been pressing the Federal Government and its executive branches and Administration on Aging for the kinds of services that old people need and want. Another very important resource for churches is the weekly newsletter of the National Senior Citizens Law Center in Los Angeles. This center is staffed by lawyers who are working in the public interest. They are the backup legal council for community legal aid societies and legal services across the country. They're very cognizant about all kinds of legislative matters. pensions, social security, health rights, guardianship, and a variety of other issues that concern the elderly.

Our overall aim in the church's social witness is to affirm the contribution of older persons to our society and to draw upon their accumulated experience, skills, and wisdom in working for a society with more just access to its goods and services.

6. *The church and the dying.* As a part of ministry, the church should be educating its members about death with dignity and the right to die with dignity. Many congregations are encouraging their members to sign the Living Will and to discuss as a congregation its several provisions. It's a very important document directed to the family, physician, lawyer, and clergy. The Living Will can be found on page 111.

E: What's the legal status of that document?

M: It's not a probate document, except in the State of California. In the summer of 1976, Governor Brown signed into law an instrument that makes it possible for people to decide in advance to sign a document instructing those who survive that there should be no artificial or extraordinary means used to extend or prolong life when it is reasonably clear that death is imminent. The mandate is to absolve the survivors of any feelings of guilt. This is a free and responsible decision on the part of the person about his or her demise. It seems to me that this is a very important instrument to discuss in the congregation in appropriate ways and to have as many people as possible in the congregation sign it, and also to work with the courts and with bar associations to get this kind of document legally binding in all fifty states.

E: Besides the Living Will, what other practices ought the church to favor and develop regarding the terminally ill? For example, I'm convinced that a lot of people who visit the terminally ill on behalf of the deacons, or some other group, are really not prepared to carry out a constructive role.

M: It's often a shock to people who visit someone who shows great weakness, physical deterioration, and mental confusion. This is a task that needs some preparation and some understanding of the finitude of everyone. We all have to die and we should accept this as a part of life.

E: It seems to me that there should be as much special training for that role as there is for the counseling role, if we envision lay people doing that.

M: I would hope that this would be very much on the church's agenda. A final aspect of this very important and critical subject is the support that increasing numbers of churches are giving to the organizing of memorial societies, investigating the practices of local funeral directors and pressing for disclosure of their fees. There ought to be some agreement on the part of funeral directors as to limitation on costs. The emphasis ought to be on memorial services rather than glorification of the corpse. There ought to be encouragement to have very simple burials in plain pine boxes or cremation, as well as arranging for certain parts of the body to be donated for medical research. A memorial society is a democratic nonprofit association of people formed to obtain dignity, simplicity, and economy in funeral arrangements. Experience has taught us that simplicity can reduce both suffering and expense at time of death. Grief is not measured by the size of the funeral or the expense of the casket!
Memorial societies have been formed in forty-one states, often through the leadership of church members. Information may be secured from the Continental Association of Funeral and Memorial Societies, Suite 1100, 1828 L Street, N.W., Washington, DC 20036.

E: I believe that Jessica Mitford pointed out a few years ago that the funeral industry had successfully lobbied to require embalming in some states, even when there is cre-

A LIVING WILL

To My Family, My Physician, My Lawyer, My Clergyman

To Any Medical Facility in Whose Care I Happen to Be

To Any Individual Who May Become Responsible for My Health, Welfare, or Affairs

Death is as much a reality as birth, growth, maturity and old age —it is the one certainty of life. If the time comes when I,_____ _____ can no longer take part in decisions for my own future, let this statement stand as an expression of my wishes, while I am still of sound mind.

If the situation should arise in which there is no reasonable expectation of my recovery from physical or mental disability, I request that I be allowed to die and not be kept alive by artificial means or "heroic measures." I do not fear death itself as much as the indignities of deterioration, dependence, and hopeless pain. I, therefore, ask that medication be mercifully administered to me to alleviate suffering even though this may hasten the moment of death.

This request is made after careful consideration. I hope you who care for me will feel morally bound to follow its mandate. I recognize that this appears to place a heavy responsibility upon you, but it is with the intention of relieving you of such responsibility and of placing it upon myself in accordance with my strong convictions that this statement is made.

Signed_____

Date_____
Witness_____
Witness_____
Copies of this request
have been given to_____
_____

Prepared by the Euthanasia Educational Council,
250 West 57th Street, New York, NY 10019

mation. What do you think should be the church's position?

M: The Gray Panthers joined in a series of hearings that the Federal Trade Commission had on funeral practices. Not too many people testified. The Gray Panthers presented some evidence of the expense of funerals, the way in which the grief of the survivors is exploited, etc. Since then, some funeral practices have been investigated; many funeral directors now offer the option of inexpensive funerals and simple burials. The churches should be lobbying for this and insisting that the funerals which they have a part in arranging meet these new and human standards.

7. *The church's position toward retirement and nursing homes.* Church members are often admitted to nursing homes when their families can no longer care for them. Some of the nursing homes are church-related. The nursing home scene has not been a pleasant one. Newspapers have exposed all kinds of abuses and neglect of patients, along with the exorbitant prices and profits that the nursing home industry has been able to realize. We believe that the nursing home industry (with some marked exceptions) will not appreciably change without vigilance on the part of churches and community groups; and we would hope that the church would take some initiative in organizing not just friendly visitors who will go on a one-to-one basis to see residents, but who will really organize the residents and families of residents for their own welfare and act as advocates.

Many local churches, as well as judicatories, are administratively responsible for retirement and nursing homes. The church needs to be aware of the rights of the residents and to take steps to ensure their well-being. Many churches will form groups of officers and members, including young and old, to work on task forces on aging so that there can be some continuing interaction with the residents of retirement and nursing homes. I often wonder why it took Ralph Nader and two young college students to blow the whistle on the nursing home scene, when for decades ministers and lay people have been visiting extended-care facilities as a part of their pastoral ministry.

E: Apparently it must have something to do with a limited definition of "ministry" as primarily being one-on-one, person-to-person, without concern for the structural issues involved.

M: It's hard to believe that a consistent visitor in a particular facility wouldn't be aware of the quality of care and what was needed to secure it and to affirm good care when it was apparent.

8. *The use of church facilities for clinics, multipurpose centers, nutrition sites, etc.* We would like to get some books and magazines made available in those places where old people come for hot lunches, but that's hard to do, because the guidelines don't call for that. The primary business is to get the food hot, get it served on time, get people in and get them out. If you have a nutrition site in your church, you could introduce people to books and new ideas. I have a feeling it might lift the level of interest and morale of the constituents and the staff.

E: A production-line mentality can become habitual. An acquaintance tells me that a lot of retired folks come to the local church family night supper; but if the church doesn't have a specific program that begins right when the dishes are cleared, they're ready to leave. Generally they're not going anyplace. But to get them just to lean back in their chairs and talk to one another requires some intervention techniques.

M: Another thing that's interesting is that some people go the rounds of the nutrition sites. They know that they have good food at a certain place on Monday and at another place on Tuesday. The nutrition sites have a large educational task in addition to providing food. Moreover, they should be helping to organize food co-ops and community gardens.

E: To me one of the more insidious developments is the legalization of bingo. Playing bingo has gone beyond the realm of occupying time.

M: You're absolutely right. There are a lot of multipurpose centers that are more than food distribution sites, where people come for the day and the principal activity is bingo. It's very easy to get a big, warm-body count where you have bingo games going on—nothing interferes with the bingo game. We're perpetuating the mindlessness.

E: This becomes a challenge to the church. One church I know of takes its turn a week at a time serving the food in the soup line. Instead of sending a group down just to feed them, they have an intergenerational committee that presents a program as well.

M: One of the things that works quite well, especially if there's a turnover, is introducing yourself to some of the people in the line—just interviewing with such questions as: Where are you from? What did you do? They then start talking with one another, and the motivation to get involved (at least in this way) builds. You just have to get them started.

9. *Setting up a task force on aging.* A task force on aging ought to have some ongoing responsibilities recognized by the pastor and officers of the church, and there ought to be a small working budget assigned for its work. It should be action-oriented as well as concerned for adequate services. Much of its work and strategy should be directed to changing some of the corporate structures of our society and the church. Congregations have much more clout and influence than they sometimes recognize.

The pastor(s) and officers of the church have a specific role as formal leaders—to enable, energize, and motivate emerging natural leaders from the group and give them full opportunity to develop, grow, and exercise leadership.

E: What are some of the areas of work for such a task force?

M: The local task force on aging could obviously begin with an age study of the congregation. It would be interesting for the congregation to know the age span of their members—who are the youngest and who are the oldest, and where they live. Usually the older members live closer to the church and are not too apt to be fully involved in the life of the church. They're isolated, even from the church. The government offices—the area offices on aging—and community services of various kinds have outreach workers who are supposed to find the isolated elderly, people who have locked themselves in one-room apartments and who are afraid to come out; but the church often has these people on their membership rolls and ought to be seeking them if they don't come out themselves.

E: So we do this particular age profile, which I imagine most congregations have. What then?

M: A lot of people are very discouraged that the age pyramid shows relatively few members who are young and a growing group of people who are old. They're despairing about the church's future, and feel that they're losing ground. If the survey could also include some assessment of the experience of people in their later years, the task force on aging could build a skill bank, begin to identify the skills that are needed by the congregation and the community, and encourage older members to be very much a part of community change and community action.

E: Have you noticed that very few people over sixty-five teach Sunday school, except the adult Bible classes?

M: Yes. And it would be marvelous if older people were teaching the very young ones. Many children in our congregations today live far away from their grandparents. There are a variety of new "foster grandparent" roles that the older members of congregations could play in relation to the younger members, particularly teen-agers who are often isolated and alienated from their families. People of their grandparents' age might be able to be more understanding and have more time.

E: Would the task force on aging have an issue focus primarily, or would it try to think in terms of training people to take on certain roles?

M: Both. Some of the issues are poverty, income maintenance, unavailability and expense of quality health care,
housing; all of those very practical issues have to be dealt
with in social action strategy. Beyond that, there is the enabling role to help retired people to move to new kinds of
jobs which begin to use the experience and accumulated
skills of older Americans and deploy them in a variety of
new jobs that our society really needs. Possible jobs are in
hospitals and nursing homes. We've defined the patient advocate as someone who could be very helpful in emergency
wards and clinics, by being at the side of the patient and
identifying his or her needs and seeing that care is given.
There is a great deal to be done to reform the courts and our
penal system. People who have time and experience ought
to devote some time during every week to watch the courts,
learn all they possibly can about criminal justice and injustice, visit correctional facilities, and provide some continuing friendship and counsel to the people who are released
offenders.

We'd like to see many people, particularly those who are
homebound or physically immobile, be media watchers.
We have a Gray Panthers "media watch" priority, which is
developing criteria for viewing prime-time television—local
stations as well as the network programs—commending
programming that is not agist or sexist or violent, complain-
ing about the way in which much of the media programming
depicts age and also about the commercials which are pretty
demoralizing and demeaning. We were able, as Gray Panthers, to get the Good Broadcasting Code of the National
Association of Broadcasters amended to include a restraint
on programming that is objectionable from an age point of
view. Now it remains to be seen whether or not that code
is followed.

We'd like to see retired clergy prepare themselves to be

ethical counselors in stockholders' meetings and to corporate management. The great corporations, particularly national ones, have a large debt to society and lots of practices that pollute the earth and the waters, that make unbridled profits, and that oppress workers. Those practices ought to be known to the stockholders, and stockholders ought to be pressing for corporate accountability.

E: Why do you single out clergy for this role?

M: Well, it's something that shouldn't be restricted to the clergy, but it just seems like an appropriate thing that ministers might want to do. For one thing, they have certain recognized credentials to raise the moral issues, to keep ethical issues on the agenda, and to be aware themselves, as students of ethics and moral values in society, of constructive ways corporate power can be used. The churches have had some success, through the National Council of Churches, in monitoring the way in which church investments are made. We've made some very important points on that score and more of it should be done.

10. *Pressing for change in seminary education.* The local church ought to be pressing for changes in seminary education. Theological education in general gives very little attention to pastoral ministries, or the role of ministers with regard to aging members of their congregation. Ministers could avoid the discouragement and lack of competence that many of them have felt if there were some preparation for these kinds of ministries in seminary education. There should be dialogue between the churches and seminary faculty who are concerned about ethics, particularly social ethics. We should be pressing in churches for some good

theological undergirding of these new ministries. Biblical-theological awareness ought to be part of seminary theological education today.

E: That's a helpful summary of the task of the church. But very few local churches would feel that they have enough expertise by themselves to do those ten things. If they utilize the resources of a larger judicatory—whether it be a district, a presbytery, a diocese, a conference, or an association—maybe it would be easier to think about developing a program. What would be the special contribution of a presbytery, or similar judicatory in other denominations, in helping congregations develop this kind of ministry?

M: Presbyteries ought to be providing ongoing training. There ought to be a series of workshops, at least annually, for ministers and lay people of the churches. There could be deployment of roles. Certain churches, with their own geographical basis and membership, could give special attention to one or several of the roles. Within the judicatory's oversight and coordinating role, all of these ten, plus other functions, could probably be developed. I would hope that the judicatory would be working on an ecumenical basis too. Much more could be done on an interfaith basis if congregations and judicatories were committed to serious ministries. Meanwhile, don't overlook the resources already in the congregation and the community.

The laity ought to play a major role in all of the various tasks of the church. They know the anxiety of retirement. The women know how difficult it is to live with a husband who is going through the trauma of separating from a lifetime career. And who knows better how to deal with the death of a spouse than does a widow or widower. From an empathetic point of view, lay people have something very special to give. The church's task in dealing with the anxieties, the fears, and the myths that have grown up in our society about growing old and being old could be described as countercultural—going against the societal stream which declares that old people are surplus, wastefolk, not useful anymore in producing profit or goods. They have a sense of history. They have demonstrated, in their own survivorship, what it takes to cope and survive in the face of change; and the church has a unique role in identifying the kinds of ministry that seem to me to be clearly needed.

E: One of the problems I see in this area of ministry is that the church is tempted to hire people to do the work or to leave it to the full-time church staff. What is your view of that pattern?

M: If the church falls into this trap, the church is merely mirroring society's assumption that old people have nothing to give and that only somebody who's professionally trained in ministries has anything to offer. I'd like to think that the older members of congregations, in their own existential situation, have a great deal to give and that they should be the ones who define the goals and work out the kinds of ministries to be done by the church. Maybe people who have retired from their jobs, and who are themselves in their later years, might be the ones who would carry out these new tasks. They certainly should be intimately involved in determining the work of the congregation. If we're honest and serious about the makeup of the local congregation, there are many kinds of human resources available to us.

The church must launch a massive attack on agism in all its oppressive and constraining forms. Congregations and judicatories have perpetuated age-segregated housing ghettos. Church boards and agencies have continued the wasteful policies of society in requiring mandatory retirement of their staff members. Theological education itself must change to equip students in various fields with the knowledge and skill they need to reach older persons in the worshiping community.

We need to enlist the help of liberation theologians, Bible scholars, Christian ethicists, and church educators in sensitizing both church and society to the damage that agism does to people and groups. Biblical and theological perspectives are essential to support the changes that must come to congregational life and outreach.

A second Reformation waits in the wings!

VIII.
CONCLUSION

All of this sure beats Geritol!—M. K.

M: There have been two prevailing theories of how to age successfully. For twenty-five years the gerontology movement was run by the *disengagement theory.* You withdrew at your own rate on your own time frame from what you did when you were younger. You did this in deference to your aging body and failing physical strength. Then the gerontologists realized that that wasn't doing too well and launched into the *activities theory.* What you did in old age was an extension of the activities of middle age. Although the disengagement theory has been largely discredited, it has been firmly embedded in public policy—especially in age-segregated housing and in the present service programs, which assume that people have no power and which keep them powerless and disengaged. The majority of old people, if you ask them now, will say that they "don't want any kind of responsibility." "I deserve to take it easy. I earned it." It's been a very useful rationale for arbitrary retirement, for all of the ways in which we waste people. We don't like the activities theory either, because we think that in old age there ought not to be frenetic activity, but rather more time for life review and reflection that points to the future. We should allow for a shifting of gears to move in a new direction where we can take on the roles of advocate and social critic, and become the responsible elder of society. We don't have a theory for that. Several young Gray Panthers are beginning to develop a theoretical frame of reference that the movement needs. Nor do we have a theology. The movement has not been spelled out in religious-theological terms, but there is a strong ethical-moral base in our social analysis and social strategy. We are deeply committed to efforts to humanize our society in the light of Biblical teaching about social justice.

The possibility of developing new theories about aging and a new theological-ethical understanding of age is an important goal for the churches. I think it's crucial that we combine sound social analysis and reflective thought and action, as is exemplified in the work of liberation theologians. What we do in any kind of action, social protest, or demonstration in the streets should be based on accurate information and facts understood by the participants. You have to do your homework or you'd better not be out on that picket line. Some of the demonstrations that have engaged senior citizens have been using the Alinsky style of organizing, where the homework and strategy are done by the organizers. Warm, live bodies have been loaded into buses and whizzed to state capitols, and it's a great picnic; but they don't know too much about why they're going. This is irresponsible organizing, because the people involved in the action ought to know the basis of it. They ought to be part of working out the strategy of it. The process should radicalize and increase political awareness. The educative process of getting our heads straight and building community is essential.

S: My impression from the last few days with you is that the view of aging you're presenting is certainly more holistic than the disengagement or activities theories. Perhaps the theory is: *multiple and diversified growth.*

M: That's a good summary. It is holistic. We think of the whole life-span. Life is a process of continuing growth. I hope we also see people not just as they are affected by an issue like housing or mandatory retirement, but that we see people in the context of their personal/societal living situation. The human condition joins the issues and the people. You can't separate any one of them in the social context. We believe very much in coalitions. One of the issues that we're just attempting to forge is with the handicapped and the mentally retarded. We think that there would be tremendous political power in that too. They can be their own advocates for access to education, public transportation, health care, etc. All of life is a gift. I think that the programs that waste it, trivialize it, and reduce it to disengagement are under judgment—the mandate of the gospel. Certainly what we know about the Old Testament concept of justice is clearly to be affirmed in these times.

S: Are there any courses on aging presently being offered in the seminaries?

M: Very few that offer more than a little gerontological content. The medical schools are doing better than the theological schools at this point. Some medical faculties say that's because we have raised the questions with them. Many retired ministers and lay people should be reeducating themselves and taking on new roles, doing new kinds of public interest work. They could become consultants to seminaries, patient advocates, ethical counselors in public decisions, etc., instead of petering out their lives. Aging should be a transitional phase, rather than a phasing out. Several of our Gray Panther leaders who are ministers still on the rolls of a presbytery, a district, or conference, say that again and again they are fighting the battle against arbitrary retirement in churches. We believe that you don't retire from life, which is what retirement now means, but that you recycle and redirect your goals. This is a component of continuing education. A special effort ought to be made to extend continuing education to provide opportunities for retired people to become involved again in the life of their community. Every one of us has a public duty to answer these questions:

1. What do you plan to do with the rest of your life?
2. What do you want your neighborhood to be like in the next five years? Who will take responsibility for changing/conserving it?
3. Who should plan the future? What work must be done to guarantee the future?
4. What new processes and institutions are needed for human goals? for the well-being of the people?

I believe we stand precariously on the brink—we have the capacity to destroy our society or to heal and humanize it. Many new ideas are to be tested. Each of us has some influence, a platform. America suffers from rampant ennui. Old people often have an exaggerated case of inertia linked with cynicism, loneliness, and despair. Much of the despair will lift when we realize that the power ultimately is in the people.

We are the stewards of our lives. We are the futurists!

How do we keep ourselves alive and contributing to our society?

How do we motivate our peers who have copped out? How do we get back into the mainstream?

S: Maggie, our time together is about gone and I don't want to close without affirming the new niche and new role and new career that you've made for yourself and how much we all appreciate you.

M: It's been a lovely week for me. I hope we can keep in touch and I look forward to seeing many of you again. I encourage you the young and middle-aged to realize that this is a revolutionary thing that we're into. It can change all of society for the foreseeable future, with impact on generations to come.

S: You have given me a new mind-set on aging. I especially like the way you model what you teach. You are your best subject matter.

M: Oh, that's a very high tribute. I appreciate that, and each one of you.

BIBLIOGRAPHY

I. Introduction—Age in a New Age

Butler, Robert N., "Toward a Psychiatry of the Life Cycle,"
   in Leon J. Epstein and Alexander Simon (eds.), *Aging in
   Modern Society.* Washington, DC: American Psychiatric
   Association, 1968.
———*Why Survive? Being Old in America,* pp. 1–63. New
   York: Harper & Row, Publishers, Inc., 1975.
Campbell, Thomas C., "O, for Christ's Sake, a Whole Issue
   on Old People," *The Christian Ministry,* March 1971, p.
   6.
"The Elderly in America," *Population Bulletin,* Vol. 30, No.
   3, 1976.
U.S. Department of Commerce, Bureau of the Census,
   *Demographic Aspects of Aging and the Older Popula-
   tion in the United States.* Current Population Reports,
   Special Studies Series, P–23, No. 56, May 1976.

128

II. Life Review

Butler, Robert N., "The Life Review: An Interpretation of Reminiscences in the Aged," *Psychiatry,* 26 (1963), pp. 65–76.

———"Successful Aging and the Role of Life Review," *Journal of the American Geriatrics Society,* December 1974, pp. 529–535.

Fairchild, Roy, *Life-Story Conversations: Dimensions in a Ministry of Evangelistic Calling.* New York: United Presbyterian Program Area on Evangelism, 475 Riverside Drive, 1977.

Kramlinger, Thomas, "Life Stories: An Aid to Life Meanings," in John T. Kelly (ed.), *Perspectives on Human Aging,* pp. 37–47. Minneapolis: Craftsman Press, 1976.

Lewis, Charles N., "The Adaptive Value of Reminiscing in Old Age," *Journal of Geriatric Psychiatry,* 6 (1973), pp. 117–121.

Lewis, Myrna I., and Butler, Robert N., "Life Review Therapy," *Geriatrics,* 29 (1974), pp. 165–173.

Myerhoff, Barbara G., and Tufts, Virginia, "Life History as Integration: An Essay on an Experimental Model," *The Gerontologist,* December 1975, pp. 541–543.

Zeiger, Betty L., "Life Review in Art Therapy with the Aged," *American Journal of Art Therapy,* January 1976, pp. 47–50.

III. Playpens and Warehouses: Retirement Communities and Homes

Brody, Elaine M.; Kleban, Morton H.; and Liebowitz, Bernard, "Intermediate Housing for the Elderly," *The Gerontologist,* August 1975, pp. 350–356.

Butler, Robert N., *Why Survive? Being Old in America,* pp.

103–138, 260–299. New York: Harper & Row, Publishers, Inc., 1975.

Curtin, Sharon R., *Nobody Ever Died of Old Age.* Boston: Little, Brown & Company, Inc., 1973.

Griesel, Elma, and Horn, Linda, *Citizens' Action Guide: Nursing Home Reform.* Philadelphia: Gray Panthers, April 1975. 4th printing, July 1976.

Horn, Linda, and Griesel, Elma, *Nursing Homes: A Citizens' Action Guide.* Boston: Beacon Press, Inc., 1977.

Jacobs, Jerry, *Older Persons and Retirement Communities: Case Studies in Social Gerontology.* Springfield, IL: Charles C Thomas, Publisher, 1975.

McFarland, M. Carter, "The Emergence of a New Concept —Congregate Housing for the Elderly," *Aging,* February-March 1976, pp. 7–10.

Mendelson, Mary Adelaide, *Tender Loving Greed.* New York: Alfred A. Knopf, Inc., 1974.

Nader, Ralph, Study Group Reports, *Old Age: The Last Segregation: The Report on Nursing Homes,* by Claire Townsend. New York: Grossman Publishers, 1971.

National Council on Aging, *A Guide for Selection of Retirement Housing.* Washington, DC: National Council on Aging, 1976.

Shore, Herbert, "The Residents' Bill of Rights—Revisited," *Concern in Care of Aging,* February-March 1976, pp. 19–22.

Turbow, Sandra R., "Geriatric Group Day Care and Its Effect on Independent Living: A Thirty-six Month Assessment," *The Gerontologist,* December 1975, pp. 508–510.

U.S. Department of Housing and Urban Development, Library and Information Division, *The Built Environment for the Elderly and the Handicapped: A Bibliography.* Washington, DC: Government Printing Office, June 1971.

U.S. Senate Special Committee on Aging, *Alternatives to*

Nursing Homes: A Proposal. Prepared by Levinson Gerontological Policy Institute, Brandeis University, Waltham, MA. Washington, DC: Government Printing Office, October 1971.

U.S. Senate Subcommittee on Long Term Care, *Nursing Home Care in the United States: Failure in Public Policy.* Washington, DC: Government Printing Office, 1974.

IV. HEALTH

Butler, Robert N., *Why Survive? Being Old in America,* pp. 174–224. New York: Harper & Row, Publishers, Inc., 1975.

Dowling, Michael, *Health Care in the Church.* Philadelphia: United Church Press, 1977.

Galton, Lawrence, *Don't Give Up on an Aging Parent.* New York: Crown Publishers, Inc., 1974.

Ehrenreich, Barbara and John, *The American Health Empire: Power, Profits, and Politics: A Report from the Health Policy Advisory Center.* A Health-PAC Book. New York: Random House, Inc., 1970.

Harmer, Ruth Mulvey, *American Medical Avarice.* New York: Abelard-Schuman, Ltd., 1974.

Illich, Ivan, *Medical Nemesis: The Expropriation of Health.* New York: Pantheon Books, 1976.

Institute for Policy Studies, Community Health Alternative Project, *Questions and Answers on a National Community Health Service.* Washington, DC: Institute for Policy Studies, 1976. 6 pages.

Madison, Terry Mizrahi, *The American Health System: A Consumer and Action Guide.* Charleston, WV: Appalachian Research and Defense Fund, 1976.

————*Organizing for Better Community Health: Programs and Strategies for Consumer Health Groups.* Charleston, WV: Appalachian Research and Defense Fund, 1976.

131

—————The People's Right to Good Health: A Guide to Consumer Health Rights and Their Enforcement. Charleston, WV: Appalachian Research and Defense Fund, 1976.

Quinn, Joan L., "Triage: Coordinated Home Care for the Elderly," Nursing Outlook, September 1975, pp. 570–573.

Rutstein, David D., The Coming Revolution in Medicine. Cambridge, MA: The MIT Press, 1967.

Trager, Brahna, "Home Care: Providing the Right to Stay Home," Hospitals, October 16, 1975, pp. 93–98.

U.S. Congress, Congressional Budget Office, Budget Options for Fiscal Year 1977. A Report to the Senate and House Committees on the Budget, Part II–1, Section B, Health (Function 550). Washington, DC: Congressional Budget Office, March 15, 1976.

U.S. Department of Health, Education and Welfare, Social Security Administration, Office of Research and Statistics, "Main Features of Selected National Health Care Systems," Research and Statistics Note, May 18, 1973, pp. 1–5.

U.S. House of Representatives Subcommittee on Health and Long Term Care, Comprehensive Home Health Care: Recommendations for Action, November 10, 1975. Washington, DC: Government Printing Office, 1976.

V. Mandatory Retirement

Adler, Joan, The Retirement Book: A Complete Early-Planning Guide to Finances, New Activities, and Where to Live. New York: William Morrow & Company, Inc., 1975.

American Medical Association, Retirement: A Medical Phi-

132

losophy and Approach. Chicago, IL: American Medical Association, 1972.

Clague, Ewan; Palli, Balraj; and Kramer, Leo, *The Aging Worker and the Union.* New York: Praeger Publishers, 1971.

Cobb, Sidney and Kasl, "Some Medical Aspects of Unemployment," *Industrial Gerontology,* Winter 1972, pp. 8–15.

Eglit, Howard, "Is Compulsory Retirement Constitutional?" *The Civil Liberties Review,* Fall 1974, pp. 87–97.

Geist, Harold, *The Psychological Aspects of Retirement.* Springfield, IL: Charles C Thomas, Publisher, 1968.

Gillian, Robert, "The Federal Age Discrimination in Employment Act Revisited," *The Clearinghouse Review,* March 1976.

Harris, Louis, and Associates, Inc., *The Myth and Reality of Aging in America.* Washington, DC: National Council on Aging, 1975.

Jaffee, A. J., "The Retirement Dilemma," *Industrial Gerontology,* Summer 1972, pp. 1–89.

Meier, Elizabeth L., "Over 65: Expectations and Realities of Work and Retirement," *Industrial Gerontology,* Spring 1975, pp. 95–100.

O'Neill, Nena and George, *Shifting Gears: Finding Security in a Changing World.* New York: M. Evans and Company, 1974.

Schulz, James, "The Economics of Mandatory Retirement," *Industrial Gerontology,* Spring 1975.

Server, Alan M., "Mandatory Retirement at Age 65—A Survey of the Law," *Industrial Gerontology,* Winter 1974, pp. 11–22.

Slavick, Fred, *Compulsory and Flexible Retirement in the American Economy.* Ithaca, NY: Cornell University Press, 1966.

"Strong Protest Against Forced Retirement," *Nation's Business,* July 1976, pp. 14–15.

Woodring, Paul, "Why 65? The Case Against Mandatory Retirement," *Saturday Review,* Aug. 7, 1976, pp. 18–20.

VI. CHANGING LIFE-STYLES

Alpaugh, Patricia K.; Renner, V. Jayne; and Birren, James E., "Age and Creativity: Its Implications for Education and Teachers," *Educational Gerontology,* January-March 1976, pp. 17–40.

Bart, Pauline B., *et al., No Longer Young: The Older Woman in America.* Ann Arbor: Institute of Gerontology, 1975.

Beresford, John C., *et al., Living in the Multigenerational Family.* Ann Arbor: Institute of Gerontology, 1969.

Butler, Robert N., and Lewis, Myrna I., *Sex After Sixty: A Guide for Men and Women for Their Later Years.* New York: Harper & Row, Publishers, Inc., 1976.

Clavan, Sylvia, and Vatter, Ethel, "The Affiliated Family: A Device for Integrating Old and Young," *The Gerontologist,* Winter 1972, pp. 407–412.

De Crow, Roger, *New Learning for Older Americans: An Overview of National Effort.* Washington, DC: Adult Education Association, 1975.

Havighurst, Robert J., "Education Through the Adult Life Span," *Educational Gerontology,* January-March 1976, pp. 41–51.

Hougland, Kenneth, "Liberation from Age-ism: The Ministry of Elders," *The Christian Century,* March 24, 1974.

Hudson Guild–Hudson Guild Fulton Senior Association, *Cafe–Co-op, Inc.: A Cooperative Approach to Food for the Elderly—A Final Report.* Washington, DC: Department of Health, Education and Welfare, Social and

Rehabilitation Service, Administration on Aging, August 1971.

Hyman, Stanley D., "Changing Careers in Midstream," *Manpower,* June 1975, pp. 22–26.

Kuhn, Margaret, "Elders in the City—A Celebration," *The Christian Ministry,* November 1972, pp. 36–39.

"Older Worker: Issues in Second Careers," *Industrial Gerontology,* Spring 1976, pp. 83–103.

Parker, Pamela L. (ed.), *Understanding Aging.* Philadelphia: United Church Press, 1974.

Shanks, Ann Zane, *Old Is What You Get: Dialogues on Aging by the Old and the Young.* New York: The Viking Press, Inc., 1976. Photographs by the author.

Sommers, Tish, *The Not-So-Helpless Female: How to Change Things Around You—Even If You Never Thought You Could.* New York: David McKay Company, Inc., 1973.

Streib, Gordon, and Streit, Ruth B., "Communes and the Aging: Utopian Dream and Gerontological Reality," *American Behavioral Scientist,* December 1975, pp. 176–189.

VII. THE CHURCH'S CONTINUING ROLE WITH THE AGING

Butler, Robert N., "Toward Practical Ecumenism," *Bulletin of the American Protestant Hospital Association,* 34 (1970), pp. 6–12.

Clingan, Donald F., *Aging Persons in the Community of Faith: A Guidebook for Churches and Synagogues on Ministry to, for, and with the Aging.* Indianapolis: The Institute on Religion and Aging, 1975.

Comfort, Alex, *A Good Age.* New York: Crown Publishers, Inc., 1976.

Harris, Louis, and Associates, Inc., *The Myth and Reality of*

Aging in America. Washington, DC: National Council on Aging, 1975.

Hiltner, Seward, *Toward a Theology of Aging.* New York: Behavioral Publications, Inc., 1975.

Kerschner, Paul A. (ed.), *Advocacy and Age: Issues, Experiences, Strategies.* Los Angeles: University of Southern California Press, 1976.

Kuhn, Margaret E., *Get Out There and Do Something About Injustice.* New York: Friendship Press, 1972.

Longino, Charles F., Jr., and Kitson, Gay C., "Parish Clergy and the Aged: Examining Stereotypes," *Journal of Gerontology,* May 1976, pp. 340–345.

Rodstein, Manuel, "Challenging Residents to Assume Maximal Responsibilities in the Homes for the Aged," *Journal of the American Geriatrics Society,* July 1975, pp. 317–321.

Synagogue Council of America, *That the Days May Be Long in the Good Land: A Guide for Aging Programs for Synagogues.* New York: Synagogue Council of America, 1975.

Walters, Elinor; Fink, Sylvia; and White, Betty, "Peer Group Counseling for Older People," *Educational Gerontology,* April-June 1976.

VIII. CONCLUSION

Binstock, Robert, "Aging and the Future of American Politics," *The Annals of the American Academy of Political and Social Science,* September 1974, pp. 199–211.

Butler, Robert N., *Why Survive? Being Old in America,* pp. 321–355, 384–422. New York: Harper & Row, Publishers, Inc., 1975.

Glenn, Norval D., "Aging, Disengagement and Opinionation," *Public Opinion Quarterly,* Spring 1969, pp. 17–33.

Kerschner, Paul A. (ed.), *Advocacy and Age: Issues, Experiences, Strategies.* Los Angeles: University of Southern California Press, 1976.

Kline, Chrysee, "The Socialization Process of Women: Implications for a Theory of Successful Aging," *The Gerontologist,* December 1975, pp. 486–492.

Lowenthal, Marjorie Fiske, *et al., Four Stages of Life.* San Francisco: Jossey-Bass, Inc., Publishers, 1975.

Markham, Elizabeth W., "Disengagement Theory Revisited," *International Journal of Aging and Human Development,* Vol. VI, No. 3 (1975), pp. 183–186.

Peterson, David A.; Powell, Chuck; and Robertson, Lawrie, "Aging in America: Toward 2000," *The Gerontologist,* June 1976, pp. 264–270.

"To Be Old in America," E/SA Forum–17, in *Engage/Social Action,* May 1976.

SOME ADDRESSES

Adult Education Association, 1225 19th Street, N.W.,Washington, DC 20036.

Appalachian Research and Defense Fund, 1116–B Kanawha Boulevard East, Charleston, WV 25301.

Behavioral Publications, Inc., 72 Fifth Avenue, New York, NY 10011.

Craftsman Press, 2117 N.W. River Road, Minneapolis, MN 55414.

Friendship Press, 475 Riverside Drive, Room 772, New York, NY 10027.

Gray Panthers, 3700 Chestnut Street, Philadelphia, PA 19104.

Institute for Policy Studies, Community Health Alternative Project, 1901 Q Street, N.W., Washington, DC 20009.

Institute of Gerontology, 520 East Liberty Street, Ann Arbor, MI 48109.

Jossey-Bass, Inc., Publishers, 615 Montgomery Street, San Francisco, CA 94111.

National Council on Aging, 1848 L Street, N.W., Suite 504, Washington, DC 20036.

Synagogue Council of America, 432 Park Avenue South, New York, NY 10016.

AUDIO-VISUALS

About Aging: A Catalog of Films, compiled by Mildred V. Allyn, Project Editor. Andrus Gerontology Center, University of Southern California, Los Angeles, CA 90007.

Aging in America. Panel: Margaret E. Kuhn, The Gray Panthers; Dr. Robert N. Butler, author, *Why Survive? Being Old in America;* Arthur S. Fleming, Commissioner on the Aging, U.S. Department of Health, Education and Welfare. Tape 2 from a series of conferences held at the National Presbyterian Center in Washington, DC, on *A Moral Audit of American Society.* This one-hour cassette may be ordered from the National Presbyterian Center, 4125 Nebraska Avenue, N.W., Washington, DC 20016.

Housing Options for Older People, 16mm. film, 28 minutes, color. Created to serve as a basis of discussion for older persons and their families, it does not make judgments and it does not deal with nursing homes. Order from ETV Center, MVR Hall, Cornell University, Ithaca, NY 14935.

Journey's End, 16mm. film, 27 minutes, color. Planning for the end of life (estate, funeral, etc.). Available on loan from NRTA/AARP Regional Offices or write to NRTA/AARP Public Relations, 1909 K Street, N.W., Washington, DC 20049.

Maggie Kuhn: Wrinkled Radical, 16mm. film, 27 minutes, color. Maggie, at age seventy, is interviewed by Studs Terkel, and is shown in her work as Gray Panther convener. Order or rent from Indiana University Audio-Visual Center, Bloomington, IN 47401.

Making Retirement Constructive, 16mm. film, 15 minutes, black and white. An effective, provocative interview with Layona Glenn, still dynamically alive at 102! Order from Institute of Lifetime Learning, AARP, 1225 Connecticut Avenue, N.W., Washington, DC 20036.

A Matter of Indifference, 16mm. film, 50 minutes, black and white. A critique of our society's ambivalence toward its aged. Order from Phoenix Films, Inc., 743 Alexander Road, Princeton, NJ 08540.

May Your Years Be Long, 16mm. film, 30 minutes, black and white. Presents points of view and philosophy of several leading gerontologists about housing, preretirement planning, etc. Order from Institute of Lifetime Learning, AARP, 1225 Connecticut Avenue, N.W., Washington, DC 20036.

Nobody Ever Died of Old Age, 16mm. film, 66 minutes, color. Drawn from the bestselling book of the same title by Sharon Curtin, it re-creates a series of her real-life experiences and vivid perceptions of what it is like to be old in America today. Order from Henry Street Settlement, Arts for Living, 466 Grand Street, New York, NY 10002.

Old, Black, and Alive! 16mm. film, 28 minutes, color, guide. Seven elderly blacks share their insight, faith, and strength in a compelling documentary of aging. Order from The New Film Company, Inc., 3331 Newbury Street, Boston, MA 02115.

Old Fashioned Woman, 16mm. film, 40 minutes, color.

Kerschner, Paul A. (ed.), *Advocacy and Age: Issues, Experiences, Strategies.* Los Angeles: University of Southern California Press, 1976.

Kline, Chrysee, "The Socialization Process of Women: Implications for a Theory of Successful Aging," *The Gerontologist,* December 1975, pp. 486–492.

Lowenthal, Marjorie Fiske, *et al., Four Stages of Life.* San Francisco: Jossey-Bass, Inc., Publishers, 1975.

Markham, Elizabeth W., "Disengagement Theory Revisited," *International Journal of Aging and Human Development,* Vol. VI, No. 3 (1975), pp. 183–186.

Peterson, David A.; Powell, Chuck; and Robertson, Lawrie, "Aging in America: Toward 2000," *The Gerontologist,* June 1976, pp. 264–270.

"To Be Old in America," E/SA Forum–17, in *Engage/Social Action,* May 1976.

SOME ADDRESSES

Adult Education Association, 1225 19th Street, N.W.,Washington, DC 20036.

Appalachian Research and Defense Fund, 1116–B Kanawha Boulevard East, Charleston, WV 25301.

Behavioral Publications, Inc., 72 Fifth Avenue, New York, NY 10011.

Craftsman Press, 2117 N.W. River Road, Minneapolis, MN 55414.

Friendship Press, 475 Riverside Drive, Room 772, New York, NY 10027.

Gray Panthers, 3700 Chestnut Street, Philadelphia, PA 19104.

Institute for Policy Studies, Community Health Alternative Project, 1901 Q Street, N.W., Washington, DC 20009.

Institute of Gerontology, 520 East Liberty Street, Ann Arbor, MI 48109.

Jossey-Bass, Inc., Publishers, 615 Montgomery Street, San Francisco, CA 94111.

National Council on Aging, 1848 L Street, N.W., Suite 504, Washington, DC 20036.

Synagogue Council of America, 432 Park Avenue South, New York, NY 10016.

AUDIO-VISUALS

About Aging: A Catalog of Films, compiled by Mildred V. Allyn, Project Editor. Andrus Gerontology Center, University of Southern California, Los Angeles, CA 90007.

Aging in America. Panel: Margaret E. Kuhn, The Gray Panthers; Dr. Robert N. Butler, author, *Why Survive? Being Old in America;* Arthur S. Fleming, Commissioner on the Aging, U.S. Department of Health, Education and Welfare. Tape 2 from a series of conferences held at the National Presbyterian Center in Washington, DC, on *A Moral Audit of American Society.* This one-hour cassette may be ordered from the National Presbyterian Center, 4125 Nebraska Avenue, N.W., Washington, DC 20016.

Housing Options for Older People, 16mm. film, 28 minutes, color. Created to serve as a basis of discussion for older persons and their families, it does not make judgments and it does not deal with nursing homes. Order from ETV Center, MVR Hall, Cornell University, Ithaca, NY 14935.

Journey's End, 16mm. film, 27 minutes, color. Planning for the end of life (estate, funeral, etc.). Available on loan from NRTA/AARP Regional Offices or write to NRTA/AARP Public Relations, 1909 K Street, N.W., Washington, DC 20049.

The perspective of age. Older persons assume an active role in providing an image or model for the young. Order from Films, Inc., 1144 Wilmette Avenue, Wilmette, IL 60091.

Other People Make Me Feel Old, 16mm. film, 31 minutes, color, 3 parts. An instrument for raising consciousness about the problems associated with aging. Order from The Learning Resources Center, University of Oklahoma Health Sciences Center, P.O. Box 26901, Oklahoma City, OK 73190.

Peege, 16mm. film, 28 minutes, color. A family visits a grandmother in a nursing home at Christmas. She is blind and has lost some of her mental faculties. Order from Phoenix Films, Inc., 743 Alexander Road, Princeton, NJ 08540.

Samantha Muffin, filmstrip, 145 frames, color, 32½ minutes, cassette, script and study guide. An eighty-two-year-old mouse is remotivated by The Twelve Rejuvenating Techniques. Order from United Presbyterian Health, Education and Welfare Association, Room 1268, 475 Riverside Drive, New York, NY 10027.

That's What Living's About, 16mm. film, 18 minutes, color. A lively but philosophical look at leisure—what it means, how it affects our lives now, and how it may affect them in the future. Order from University of California Extension Media Center, Berkeley, CA 94720.

The Third Age: The New Generation, 16mm. film. The creative contribution older persons can and should be prepared to give to society through the support of the church/synagogue. For information on rental, write Audio Visual Library, P.O. Box 1986, Indianapolis, IN 46206.

We've Come of Age, 16mm. film, 12 minutes, color. Recounts the accomplishments of the generation now "old" and exhorts them to unite for their common good. Order from National Council of Senior Citizens, Film Section, 1511 K Street, N.W., Washington, DC 20005.